Wicca Spells for Beginners

A Practical Guide to Harnessing
Natural Energy

Madame Ophelia

Contents

Introduction

Hello, dear reader, and welcome. If you've picked up this book, it's likely that you're standing at the beginning of a captivating journey, a journey into the world of Wicca. You may be here out of curiosity, or perhaps a deeper yearning for a spiritual path that aligns with your profound love for nature and the universe. Whatever the case, I warmly welcome you.

Wicca, often misunderstood and misrepresented, is far more than just spellcasting and mystical rituals. It's a rich spiritual path rooted in reverence for the natural world and the unseen energies that interlace all of existence. Wicca beckons us to explore and rekindle our inherent connection to nature, guiding us to find spiritual significance in the cyclical patterns of the Earth, the phases of the moon, the changing seasons, and the intricate web of life that binds us all together.

To understand Wicca is to understand its profound bond with nature. At the heart of this path lies the principle of harmony. Just as a tree exists in harmony with the soil, the rain, the sun, and the seasons, so too are we invited to live in harmony with the world around us. Wicca encourages us to see ourselves not as separate from nature, but as an integral part of it. It teaches that each plant, stone, river, animal, and indeed every element of nature holds divine energy. It's a worldview that weaves a tapestry of interconnectedness, binding the self to the wider cosmos.

Harmony in Wicca extends to the rhythm of the natural world, too. The cycle of the seasons, the waxing and waning of the moon, the rising and setting of the sun - these natural phenomena are viewed not just as physical occurrences, but as sacred rhythms that influence the flow of energy in the world. By aligning ourselves with these rhythms, we tap into the power of the universe, grounding our practices in the ebb and flow of natural energy.

This might seem like a leap from our modern, fast-paced lives where we often feel disconnected from nature. But at its core, Wicca is a call back to our roots, a remembrance of a time when our ancestors lived in tune with the land, the skies, and the seasons. It's an invitation to slow down, to appreciate the simple and the ordinary, to witness the magic that lies in the quiet unfolding of nature.

The journey you're about to embark upon isn't just about learning how to cast spells or celebrate pagan festivals, although those aspects are indeed fascinating. It's about a transformational shift in perspective. It's about viewing the world through a lens of wonder, respect, and interconnectedness. It's about walking a path of harmony - harmony with oneself, harmony with others, and most importantly, harmony with the natural world.

Moving from the broader understanding of Wicca and its deeply woven connection with nature, we can now turn our attention to an integral component of the Wiccan path: spellcasting. If you're new to this concept, the term 'spell' might conjure up images of witches in pointy hats stirring cauldrons, or fantasy tales filled with dazzling magic and spellbound adventures. However, in the world of Wicca, spells are something far more grounded and yet wonderfully ethereal.

A Wiccan spell is, at its most basic, a focused intention. It's about aligning your will with the universe's natural energy to bring about desired change. This can range from cultivating inner peace and self-love, to attracting prosperity, to encouraging healing and protection. Spellcasting is an art of transformation, an act of co-creating your reality with the universe.

Each spell is a carefully crafted blend of elements designed to harness specific energies. These can include words of power (chants, affirmations, or rhymes), symbolic items (candles, crystals, herbs), specific timing (moon phases, days of the week), and, most importantly, a clear and focused intention. These elements, when brought together in a spell, create a powerful resonance with the energies of the universe.

However, it's essential to understand that spells aren't quick fixes or shortcuts to your desires. Wiccan spellcasting isn't about manipulating the universe or others to get what you want. It's about attuning yourself to the natural flow of the universe and manifesting changes that are in harmony with your highest good and the good of all.

The real magic of Wiccan spells lies not in the spells themselves, but in the transformative power they have on the spellcaster. Each spell you cast is a step along a path of personal growth and spiritual development. It's an opportunity to know yourself better, to delve into your own depths, and to align more closely with your true essence and the universe's rhythms.

In this book, we will delve into the world of Wiccan spellcasting. You'll learn about the different types of spells, their purposes, and the ingredients and tools used. We'll guide you through the process of casting spells, starting with simple practices and slowly moving to more complex spells as you gain confidence and understanding.

As we explore this enchanting world, remember that spellcasting is a deeply personal and spiritual practice. There's no 'one size fits all' approach here. It's about finding what resonates with you, adapting practices to fit your path, and learning to move in harmony with the natural energies of the universe.

Whether you're seeking healing, looking for love, aiming to attract prosperity, or wishing to cultivate personal growth, there's a Wiccan spell that can guide and support you on your journey. The power within these spells comes not from the words or the ingredients but from your intention, your belief, and your connection with the natural world.

Now that we've touched on the richness of the Wiccan path and the transformative potential of spellcasting, let me share a bit about myself and my journey to this point. My name is Morgan and I'm a Wiccan practitioner, teacher, and nature enthusiast. But before I stepped onto this path, I was much like you might be now - curious, seeking, and a little bit lost.

I was brought up in a traditional household, with traditional beliefs. The natural world was something to appreciate, sure, but not something with which to connect on a spiritual level. I went through life observing the beauty of nature but missing its spiritual resonance.

It wasn't until my early adulthood that I stumbled upon a book about Wicca. It was a revelation. Here was a spiritual path that revered what I'd always been drawn to - the rhythms of nature, the power of intention, the interconnectedness of all life. I delved into the Wiccan world, reading everything I could get my hands on, practicing rituals, and casting spells. I found a deep sense of connection, empowerment, and harmony that I'd never experienced before.

Over the years, my Wiccan practice has deepened and evolved. I've learned from many teachers, crafted countless spells, celebrated Sabbats under the moonlight, and experienced first-hand the transformative power of this path. Along the way, I've also become a teacher myself, guiding others who are seeking a spiritual connection with nature and the universe.

This leads me to the motivation for writing this book. I vividly remember the feelings of excitement, curiosity, and, yes, a bit of confusion when I first embarked on my Wiccan journey. I remember wishing for a guide, something that could lead me step-by-step through the unfamiliar territory of Wicca and spellcasting. As I began teaching, I saw this same need in many of my students.

So, this book is my way of guiding you through this journey. It's a collection of all the knowledge and wisdom I've gathered over the years, designed to provide a comprehensive yet accessible entry point into the world of Wicca and spellcasting. My hope is that this book will demystify Wicca, dispel misconceptions, and provide practical guidance for those eager to learn and grow on this path.

As you delve into the chapters ahead, remember that the Wiccan path is not a rigid one. It's about exploring, learning, and finding what resonates with you. It's about cultivating a personal connection with the universe and the natural world. And most importantly, it's about discovering your own inherent power to co-create your life in harmony with the greater energies of existence.

So, welcome again to this journey. May it bring you understanding, empowerment, and a deeper connection with the beautiful, magical world we live in.

Understanding Wicca

A s we delve deeper into this journey, it's important to start with a solid understanding of what Wicca truly is. Despite gaining more recognition in recent years, misconceptions about Wicca still abound. Many people, influenced by sensational media or historical biases, associate Wicca with negative stereotypes or dismiss it as mere 'witchcraft'. However, Wicca is a rich, complex, and profound spiritual path that deserves our understanding and respect.

At its core, Wicca is a modern pagan, witchcraft religion. It was developed in England during the first half of the 20th century and was introduced to the public in 1954 by Gerald Gardner, a retired British civil servant. While it's a relatively new spiritual path compared to world religions like Christianity, Islam, or Buddhism, Wicca draws on ancient pagan and hermetic motifs for its theological structure and ritual practice.

Wicca is deeply rooted in the reverence for nature and the worship of a deity that is both male and female. This religion recognizes the divinity and sacredness of all life, emphasizing harmony with nature and the universe. It's a path of balance and polarity, valuing both the masculine and feminine, light and dark, active and passive elements of life and the universe.

One of the most defining characteristics of Wicca is its flexibility and adaptability. Unlike many religions, Wicca doesn't have a rigid set of rules or a universally recognized holy text. Instead, each Wiccan practitioner is encouraged to connect with the divine in their own way, creating a spiritual path that resonates with their unique experiences and perspectives. This approach makes Wicca a deeply personal and empowering spiritual path for many people.

However, while there is considerable flexibility, there are also common beliefs and practices shared among Wiccans. These include the celebration of seasonal cycles or Sabbats, reverence for a Goddess and a God, the practice of magic and spellcasting, and the adherence to an ethical code known as the Wiccan Rede and the Threefold Law, which we will explore in more detail later in this chapter.

Wicca encourages a life of mindfulness, harmony, and respect towards all beings and the environment. It urges us to recognize the divine in everything around us, from the smallest pebble to the vast sky, and to live in harmony with the natural rhythms of the Earth. It's a path that can bring us closer to our true selves, the natural world, and the divine energy that permeates the universe.

In essence, Wicca is a spiritual path that combines reverence for nature, the practice of magic, a respect for balance and polarity, and an ethical framework to guide our actions. It's a path of empowerment, personal growth, and deep connection with the natural world and the divine."

<u>The core beliefs and principles of Wicca</u>

Wicca, like any spiritual path, is grounded in a set of core beliefs and principles. While there is considerable diversity within Wicca due to its emphasis on personal spirituality, there are some foundational beliefs shared by most Wiccans. Let's explore these in more detail.

Understanding Wicca

- **Dual Theism**: The belief in a Goddess and a God is central to most Wiccan traditions. Wiccans worship a feminine deity often associated with the Earth or Moon, and a masculine deity often associated with the Sun or sky. Some view these deities as literal beings, while others see them as symbolic representations of natural forces, life cycles, or archetypal energies. Importantly, Wiccans value the Goddess and God equally, emphasizing the balance between feminine and masculine energies in the universe.

- **Animism and Pantheism**: Many Wiccans believe in the divinity of nature and see the divine in all things – a belief known as pantheism. Coupled with this is often a perspective called animism, the view that all things (animals, plants, rocks, rivers, etc.) have a spirit or consciousness. These beliefs foster a deep respect for nature and all forms of life.

- **Magic and Witchcraft**: Wiccans believe in magic - the idea that individuals can direct natural energies to bring about change in the world around them. This is often achieved through the practice of witchcraft, which includes casting spells, performing rituals, divination, and other magical practices.

- **The Wheel of the Year**: Wiccans celebrate eight Sabbats that make up the Wheel of the Year. These include four solar festivals (the solstices and equinoxes) and four seasonal festivals. Each Sabbat is an opportunity to connect with the cycles of nature and honor the Goddess and God.

- **The Wiccan Rede and the Threefold Law**: The Wiccan Rede is a moral code that advises, 'An it harm none, do what ye will.' In other words, as long as your actions don't harm others, you're free to pursue your desires. The Threefold Law states that whatever energy a person puts out into the world, be it positive or negative, will be returned to that person three times. These principles encourage responsibility, empathy, and positive action.

- **The Afterlife and Reincarnation**: Many Wiccans believe in reincarnation, the cycle of death and rebirth. Some also believe in a realm known as the Summerland, a place of rest and rejuvenation for the soul between incarnations. However, views on the afterlife can vary greatly among Wiccans, with some focusing more on this life than speculating about what comes after.

- **Personal Autonomy and Responsibility**: Wiccans believe

in the autonomy of the individual when it comes to spiritual matters. Each person is their own spiritual authority and has the freedom to choose their beliefs, practices, and moral principles. This freedom, however, comes with responsibility. Wiccans believe individuals must take responsibility for their actions, especially when it comes to magic and ethical conduct.

These core beliefs and principles form the foundation of Wiccan practice, but it's important to remember that every Wiccan's path is unique. Wicca is a spiritual path that encourages personal exploration, growth, and the pursuit of knowledge. As you delve deeper into Wicca, you'll likely find your understanding of these principles evolving and deepening, just as your connection to the divine and the natural world will grow.

<u>A look at the deities and the reverence for nature in Wicca.</u>

Wicca places a great deal of emphasis on the divine, and this divine power is often perceived through the lens of deities, particularly a Goddess and a God. These deities are not 'supreme beings' in the sense of being above or outside the world but are immanent, intertwined with the world and the natural forces that shape it.

The Goddess is often associated with the Earth and the Moon, embodying the divine feminine. She is seen as the mother of all life, the embodiment of love, nurturing, and compassion, and is often linked with fertility, wisdom, and magic. Many Wiccans perceive the Goddess in three aspects, or faces: The Maiden, the Mother, and the Crone. Each of these aspects corresponds to a phase of the Moon and a stage of a woman's life, representing the divine feminine cyclical and ever-changing nature.

The God is usually associated with the Sun, the sky, and wild animals, embodying the divine masculine. He is seen as the Goddess's consort, a symbol of vitality, strength, and courage. The God is often represented in two primary aspects: the Horned God of life and death, who is associated with the forests and wild animals, and the Green Man, the God of vegetation and the harvest. These two aspects illustrate the God's connection to nature and the cycle of birth, death, and rebirth.

Wicca doesn't enforce strict dogma around these deities. Some Wiccans see them as literal divine beings, while others see them as symbolic representations of natural and psychological processes. They can also be viewed as aspects of a greater divine power or as archetypal figures that embody certain attributes or experiences.

Now, let's turn to the reverence for nature in Wicca. Wicca is often described as an earth-based religion due to its deep respect for the natural world. This reverence for nature is rooted in the belief that the divine permeates everything in the universe. Everything, from the grandest mountain to the smallest blade of grass, is seen as a manifestation of divine energy.

Wiccans often honor nature through their rituals and holidays. The Wheel of the Year, which represents the cycle of the seasons, is a key part of Wiccan practice. Each of the eight Sabbats (holidays) marks a stage in the seasonal cycle and provides an opportunity to connect with the rhythms of nature. Rituals often involve elements from the natural world, like herbs, stones, or symbols of animals, and they're frequently performed outdoors.

The reverence for nature also translates into a strong emphasis on environmental responsibility. Wiccans are often involved in ecological activism, and many incorporate green practices into their daily lives. Living in harmony with nature is seen not only as a spiritual responsibility but also as a vital necessity for the health and survival of our planet.

At the heart of Wicca is an intimate bond with the natural world. Through reverence for the Goddess and God and respect for nature, Wiccans cultivate a deep sense of connection with the world around them. This connection enhances their spiritual practice, fostering a sense of unity with the divine and all forms of life.

In the next section, we will explore two essential tenets of Wiccan ethics: the Wiccan Rede and the Threefold Law. These principles, combined with the core beliefs and reverence for deities and nature, provide a robust framework for Wiccan spiritual practice.

Explanation of the Wiccan Rede and the Threefold Law.

The Wiccan Rede and the Threefold Law are two key ethical guidelines in Wicca. They're not commandments or absolute rules, but rather, they're principles that encourage individual responsibility, kindness, and harmony with nature.

The Wiccan Rede is a simple, yet profound, statement: 'An it harm none, do what ye will.' The term 'Rede' comes from Old English and means advice or counsel. So, the Wiccan Rede is a piece of advice that guides Wiccans in their actions and choices. It tells them they're free to do what they want, as long as their actions don't harm others (including themselves). It's a statement that promotes personal freedom but also underscores the responsibility that comes with that freedom.

The Wiccan Rede encourages mindfulness and consideration. Before performing any action (and especially before casting any spell), a Wiccan is advised to consider the potential consequences and avoid causing harm. This principle fosters empathy, responsibility, and a focus on positive actions.

However, 'harm none' isn't always a straightforward concept. Life is complex, and sometimes harm can occur indirectly or be a matter of perspective. In such cases, Wiccans are encouraged to use their judgment, consider the broader context, and aim for the option that minimizes harm and promotes the greatest good.

Next is the Threefold Law, also known as the Law of Three or the Rule of Three. It states that whatever energy a person puts out into the world, be it positive or negative, will be returned to that person three times. Some interpret this literally, believing that any action (good or bad) will come back to them three times as strongly. Others view it more symbolically, seeing it as a reminder that our actions have consequences and that what we do to others can, in one way or another, come back to affect us.

The Threefold Law encourages Wiccans to be mindful of their actions, thoughts, and emotions. It promotes a life of kindness, love, and positivity, reminding Wiccans that these are the energies that will be returned to them. Similarly, it serves as a warning against harmful actions, negative attitudes, and malice.

Both the Wiccan Rede and the Threefold Law emphasize personal responsibility. In Wicca, there's no external divine power that punishes or rewards people for their actions. Instead, it's up to each person to choose their path and bear the consequences of their decisions. This focus on personal responsibility, coupled with a deep respect for all life, forms a unique ethical framework that guides Wiccans in their spiritual journey.

These principles extend beyond Wicca and can apply to anyone, regardless of their spiritual beliefs. They're about being aware of our actions, considering their impact, and striving to live a life of kindness, respect, and love. In Wicca, ethical living isn't just about following rules—it's a way of embodying the divine, of living in harmony with nature, and of fostering positive connections with ourselves and others.

Conclusion

As we close this chapter, it's essential to remember that Wicca, as a faith, is rich, complex, and deeply personal. Its foundation is built on a sense of reverence towards the divine and the natural world, a commitment to positive and ethical actions, and a belief in personal freedom and responsibility.

We have looked at the core beliefs and principles of Wicca, exploring the significance of the Goddess and the God, the importance of nature, and the ethical guidelines provided by the Wiccan Rede and the Threefold Law. Each element of these beliefs and practices works harmoniously together, creating a vibrant and life-affirming spiritual path that draws strength from both the natural world and the inner self.

As with the turning of the Wheel of the Year, Wicca represents a continuous journey, a cycle of learning and growth. It invites us to engage with the world with an open mind and a compassionate heart, to find our own path, and to seek truth and wisdom in our own unique ways.

Remember, the goal isn't to memorize every deity, understand every symbol, or follow every rule to the letter. The true essence of Wicca lies not in rigid dogma but in the individual's spiritual journey. It's about how you connect with the divine, how you find harmony with nature, and how you embody the principles of love, respect, and responsibility in your daily life.

If you're feeling overwhelmed, that's okay. All paths to knowledge start with a single step. There's no rush—take your time to absorb the information and reflect on what it means to you. Ask questions, do more research, and most importantly, listen to your intuition. It's your personal journey, after all.

The world of Wicca is a vast and fascinating one, full of mysteries to explore, wisdom to uncover, and experiences to savor. This is just the beginning, and we have a lot more to discover.

In the coming chapters, we'll delve deeper into the practical aspects of Wicca, starting with one of its most captivating elements: spellcasting. We will examine what spells are, how they work, and how you can begin to incorporate them into your own practice.

Remember, though, that the practice of Wicca—like any spiritual practice—is about more than just learning facts or performing rituals. It's about transformation, growth, and connecting with the divine. As you read on and learn more, keep an open mind, stay curious, and remember to enjoy the journey.

The Basics of Spellcasting

W elcome to Chapter 2, where we'll start exploring the intriguing world of Wiccan spellcasting. This chapter will provide a solid foundation for your spellcasting journey, beginning with understanding what spells are and their significant role within the practice of Wicca.

First and foremost, what is a spell? In simplest terms, a spell is a ritualized intention. It's a focused, formalized method of directing energy to bring about change. This change can be within you - shaping your thoughts, feelings, and actions - or it can affect the world around you. The beauty of a spell lies in its purposefulness. Each word, each action, and each element has a specific meaning and role to play.

Now, don't confuse Wiccan spellcasting with the depiction of spells in popular culture - no hocus-pocus or turning people into toads here! Wiccan spells are more about attuning yourself to natural energies and harnessing these energies to improve your life and the lives of others.

So, what role do spells play in Wicca? They're a crucial aspect of Wiccan practice, serving as a tool for personal transformation and a way to engage with the divine and the natural world. By casting spells, Wiccans actively participate in their spiritual journey, shaping their destiny rather than passively accepting it. They enable us to manifest our goals, realize our potential, and bring about the changes we desire.

Spells also embody Wicca's reverence for nature. Many spells involve natural elements like herbs, crystals, and candles, connecting us to the earth and the cycle of life. They're often timed to align with natural occurrences, like the phases of the moon or seasonal changes, further underscoring Wicca's belief in living in harmony with nature.

Moreover, spellcasting fosters a sense of empowerment and responsibility. It's a reminder that we have the power to shape our reality and that we're responsible for our actions and their consequences. This aligns with the Wiccan Rede and the Threefold Law, reinforcing the ethical framework that underpins Wiccan practice.

It's essential to note, however, that while spells are a significant part of Wicca, they're not the entirety of the practice. Wicca is a rich, holistic spiritual path that encompasses ethics, reverence for nature, celebration of life's cycles, personal growth, and more. Spells are one aspect of this broader tapestry, a tool to aid in spiritual development and foster a deeper connection with the divine and nature.

In the end, the power of a spell doesn't come from the specific words you say or the items you use, but from your belief in its purpose, your focus and intention, and your alignment with natural energies.

Explanation of how spells work

Understanding how spells work requires us to step back a bit and consider the broader worldview that Wicca and similar paths espouse. According to this perspective, everything in the universe is interconnected, interwoven by a web of energy or life-force that we, as conscious beings, can shape and direct.

Spells operate based on the idea that our thoughts, intentions, and actions can influence this web of energy. By focusing our will and combining it with symbolic actions, words, and objects, we can create a ripple in the energy field around us, nudging the universe in the direction of our desires.

So, how does a spell work in practice? Let's break it down into steps.

1. Setting the intention: The first step in casting a spell is to clarify what you want to achieve. This is your intention, the change you desire to bring into your life. This could be anything from finding love, securing a job, healing from an illness, or seeking peace of mind. Clarity and specificity are crucial here. The more specific your intention, the more effectively you can direct your energy towards it.

2. Preparing the space: Before starting the spell, it's important to prepare the space where you will be working. This often involves cleaning the physical space and then 'cleansing' it energetically, typically using methods such as smudging with sage or sprinkling saltwater. The aim is to create a sacred, welcoming space free of any negative or distracting energies.

3. Casting the circle: Once the space is prepared, the next step is to cast a circle, a protective barrier that keeps out any unwanted influences and keeps the energy of your spell contained until you're ready to release it. The circle also delineates a sacred space, separating the mundane world from the magical.

4. Invoking the divine: With the circle cast, you may then choose to invite the divine to witness or assist in your spell. This could involve calling upon the Goddess and the God, the elements, specific deities, or any spiritual entities that align with your personal beliefs.

5. Performing the spell: The actual spell work involves combining symbolic actions, words, and objects that align with your intention. This might include using specific colors, herbs, or crystals, reciting a written spell or incantation, and visualizing your intention as clearly as possible. The aim is to focus your energy and concentration fully on your intention.

6. Raising energy: The spell is followed by the raising of energy. This energy is what you will send out into the universe to bring your intention into reality. There are many ways to raise energy, including chanting, drumming, dancing, or simply visualizing energy building and swirling within your circle.

7. Releasing energy: At the climax of the spell, you will release the energy you've raised, sending it out into the universe to affect your desired change. This is often accompanied by a statement of intent, such as "So mote it be," or "As I will it, so shall it be."

8. Grounding: After releasing the energy, it's essential to ground yourself. This involves releasing any excess energy you've raised and haven't used, bringing yourself back to your normal state of being.

9. Closing the circle: Finally, you will close the circle, thanking and saying farewell to any entities you've invited, and symbolically closing the sacred space you opened.

Now, remember: each spell is unique, and not all spells will involve every step outlined here. What's more, the way each step is carried out can vary widely from person to person. It's crucial to adapt your spellcasting to what feels right and works best for you. This is, after all, your magic.

In the next section, we'll dive deeper into the importance of intention and focus in spellcasting, as well as providing an overview of some of the many elements that can be involved in a spell.

The importance of intention and focus in spellcasting.

As you've probably gathered from our earlier discussions, intention and focus aren't just elements of spellcasting - they are the very heart of it. They are what drives a spell, giving it direction and power. Without a clear intention and focused mind, a spell is like a car without a driver or a map: it's unlikely to get you where you want to go.

So, what is intention, exactly? In the context of spellcasting, intention refers to the goal or desire that you want to manifest through your spell. It's the change you want to bring about, the outcome you want to achieve. Your intention is the 'why' of your spell, the purpose behind the words you say and the actions you take.

Now, the importance of a clear, well-defined intention cannot be overstated. Your intention acts as a kind of spiritual compass, guiding your energy towards your desired destination. It's like a beacon, signaling to the universe what you wish to manifest. Without a clear intention, your energy can become dispersed and diluted, lessening the effectiveness of your spell.

Equally important is the moral and ethical quality of your intention. Remember the Wiccan Rede and the Threefold Law we discussed in Chapter 1? These principles urge you to consider the potential consequences of your spells and to ensure that your intentions align with the pursuit of harmlessness and the promotion of good.

So, how can you clarify your intention? Start by asking yourself what you truly want. Be as specific as you can. Then, consider why you want it. What will achieving this goal bring into your life? How will it benefit you and others? Reflecting on these questions can help you to hone your intention and align it with your deepest values and desires.

Once you've set your intention, it's time to focus. Focus is the ability to concentrate your mental and emotional energy on your intention, to the exclusion of all else. When you cast a spell, you're not just performing a ritual: you're engaging in a highly concentrated form of mental and spiritual activity.

Why is focus so important? Consider this: every day, our minds are bombarded by countless thoughts, feelings, and sensations. If we let these distract us during our spellcasting, our energy can become fragmented, reducing the power of our spells.

By focusing our minds, we bring all our energy to bear on our intention. We create a kind of laser beam of thought and desire that can pierce through the noise and chaos of everyday life and reach the heart of the universe.

So, how can you improve your focus? It starts with creating a quiet, peaceful environment for your spellcasting. This can help to minimize external distractions. Practicing mindfulness and meditation can also be beneficial, as they train your mind to stay present and concentrated.

In the act of spellcasting, visualize your intention as vividly as you can. See it in your mind's eye as already fulfilled. Feel the emotions you would feel if your desire were already manifested. This kind of sensory-rich, emotional visualization can sharpen your focus and amplify the power of your spell.

In essence, intention and focus are the magic in your magic, the dynamic duo that powers your spells. By honing your intentions and cultivating your ability to focus, you can significantly enhance the effectiveness of your spellcasting. Remember, your magic is a reflection of your inner world, and a clear, focused mind can create powerful, positive change in the world around you.

In the next section, we'll dive into the specific elements involved in a spell - the tools, symbols, and colors you can use to enrich your magical workings and amplify your intentions.

An overview of the elements involved in a spell - tools, symbols, colors, etc.

Magic, as you've come to understand by now, isn't a haphazard, willy-nilly process. It's a methodical art, a considered practice, woven together with various elements. These elements are the tools, symbols, colors, and more that you use in your spellcasting. Each one of them plays a unique role in your work, serving as a conduit for your intentions and focus.

Tools are the tangible, physical items you use during your spells. They help to focus your energy, channel your intentions, and represent various aspects of the natural world and the divine. Common tools used in Wiccan rituals include:

- **The Athame**: This is a ceremonial knife used for directing energy, not for physical cutting. It's typically associated with the element of air, representing intellect and the power of the mind.

- **The Wand**: Another tool for directing energy, the wand is often linked with the element of fire, symbolizing passion and willpower.

- **The Chalice**: Representing the element of water, the chalice is used to hold water or wine during rituals, symbolizing the goddess, fertility, and emotion.

- **The Pentacle**: A disc or plate, often inscribed with a pentagram, represents the element of earth. It symbolizes stability, material wealth, and physical manifestation.

- **The Cauldron**: Often used for burning items during rituals, the cauldron symbolizes the goddess, the womb, and the cycle of birth, death, and rebirth.

Symbols, on the other hand, are more about the metaphysical aspect of spellcasting. They represent various concepts, ideas, and energies, and can help you to connect with specific deities, spirits, or natural forces. You might draw them in the air with your athame or wand, inscribe them on candles or papers, or visualize them in your mind.

Common Wiccan symbols include:

- **The Pentagram/Pentacle**: This five-pointed star enclosed within a circle represents the five elements of earth, air, fire, water, and spirit.

- **The Triple Moon**: Symbolizing the Goddess in her aspects of maiden, mother, and crone, this symbol is a potent representation of feminine energy and power.

- **The Spiral**: Symbolizing the cyclical nature of life, death, and rebirth, the spiral can help you connect with the energy of the earth and the universe.

Colors also play a significant role in spellcasting. Each color is associated with specific energies and can be used to represent various intentions. For example:

- **Red** is often associated with passion, courage, and strength.

- **Green** can represent abundance, fertility, and growth.

- **Blue** might be used for healing, peace, and emotional understanding.

Understanding and harnessing the power of these elements can greatly enrich your spellcasting practice. They're like the paintings on an artist's palette, allowing you to color your spells with different energies and intentions.

In the next chapter, we will delve deeper into the use of tools and ingredients for spells, helping you understand the significance of each one and how you can use them in your practice.

<u>Conclusion</u>

In this chapter, we've embarked on a fascinating exploration of the fundamental components of spellcasting. We've looked at the definition and role of spells in Wicca, touched upon how spells work, and emphasized the crucial role of intention and focus. We've also introduced you to some of the most essential elements that can be incorporated into spells, including tools, symbols, and colors.

The primary purpose of this exploration has been to ground your understanding of spellcasting in solid knowledge. Wicca is a deeply rich and complex faith, and spellcasting is an integral part of that. With this foundation, we are now more prepared to delve into the practical aspects of spellcasting.

We've also touched upon the responsibility that comes with spellcasting. The importance of having clear, ethical intentions, the need for focus, and the potential impact of our actions. As we move further into our journey, these considerations should remain at the forefront of our minds.

Understanding the basics of spellcasting is similar to learning a new language. At first, it can seem overwhelming, with so many new terms, concepts, and practices to grasp. But, just like language learning, the more you immerse yourself in it, the more familiar it becomes. Each spell you cast, each ritual you perform, brings you one step closer to fluency.

You now have the keys to a door leading to a world of magic and spirituality. With them, you can unlock your potential to harness the natural energies around us and create real change in your life and the lives of others.

In our subsequent chapters, we will delve deeper into the practical aspects of spellcasting. We will look at how to use the tools and ingredients we've discussed, understand the significance of the Wiccan calendar, and guide you through casting your first spells.

But remember, it's not just about casting spells. It's about understanding the principles behind them, the energies at work, and the potential outcomes. It's about honoring and respecting the Wiccan Rede and the Threefold Law. It's about growing as a person and as a practitioner of the Craft.

So as we move on to our next chapter, take a moment to reflect on what you've learned so far. Remember, in the world of Wicca and magic, there's no rush. This is your journey, your path. Take it one step at a time, absorb the knowledge at your own pace, and most importantly, enjoy the process. The magic is, after all, in the journey as much as it is in the destination.

Tools and
Ingredients for
Spells

Now that we have a solid foundation of understanding regarding what spells are and the basics of how they work, let's dive deeper into the practical aspect of spellcasting: the tools and ingredients.

Magic, in the Wiccan sense, is about harnessing and directing natural energies to bring about change. To do this effectively, practitioners often employ a range of physical tools and ingredients. These aren't magical in and of themselves, but they serve as focal points for the practitioner's intention and aids in channeling energy.

Let's start by talking about some of the most common tools and ingredients used in Wiccan spellcasting.

Candles

Candles hold a significant place in the realm of Wicca and spellcasting, acting as powerful conduits of intention and energy. More than just a source of light, candles are seen as tools of manifestation that transform our thoughts and desires into tangible reality.

Each candle carries its own energetic frequency, which can be harnessed and directed towards our intended goal. When we light a candle with intention, its flame becomes a beacon, transmuting our thoughts into the universal energy field and calling forth the desired change. The act of candle burning symbolizes the release of our intention into the universe, embodying the essence of 'as above, so below'.

Moreover, candles are also color-coded in the Wiccan tradition. Each color corresponds to different elements, deities, astrological signs, and desired outcomes, allowing for a versatile and tailored approach to spellcasting. For instance, green candles are often used for prosperity and abundance spells, while pink can be used in love and relationship spells.

Candles are also used to invoke the elemental energy of Fire, one of the four cardinal elements in Wicca. Fire represents transformation, willpower, and creative energy. Thus, the simple act of lighting a candle sets these forces into motion.

Lastly, candles can be further enhanced with the use of inscriptions, symbols, or anointing oils, allowing practitioners to add a layer of personalization and power to their spell work. The act of carving or anointing a candle adds a physical element to our intentions, deepening our connection to the spell and the outcome we seek.

Overall, candles serve as versatile, accessible, and powerful tools in the practice of Wiccan spellcasting. When used with clear intention, respect, and understanding, they can greatly enhance the potency of our spells and our connection to the magic within and around us.

Crystals and Stones

Crystals and stones play an integral role in Wiccan practices and spellcasting due to their unique vibrational properties and associations with the Earth element. They are often considered as condensed, stable forms of energy, storing and radiating their innate frequencies which can be harnessed during spell work to amplify intentions or invoke specific energies.

Each type of crystal or stone has its own energy signature and set of symbolic associations. For instance, rose quartz is universally recognized for its connection to love and the heart chakra, making it an ideal choice for spells relating to love or emotional healing. Similarly, amethyst is associated with spiritual growth, intuition, and the Third Eye chakra, making it a great tool for spells intended to enhance psychic abilities or for deep meditation.

Moreover, the process of choosing a crystal for your spell work is an intuitive one. Some practitioners might feel drawn to a certain crystal due to its color, shape, or even the 'feeling' they get from it. This is believed to be the crystal's energy resonating with the practitioner's energy.

Crystals can be used in spellcasting in numerous ways. They can be placed on the altar as part of a spell's ingredients, carried as talismans, used to focus energy in meditation or visualization, or incorporated into a magic circle's casting for added protection and power.

However, it's important to cleanse and charge your crystals regularly to maintain their vibrational potency. This can be done in several ways such as bathing them in moonlight, burying them in the earth, or cleansing them with smoke from sage or incense.

All in all, crystals, and stones, with their earth-derived power and symbolic resonances, are invaluable assets to any Wiccan's toolkit.

Herbs

In the realm of Wiccan practices, herbs hold a special place, being attributed with powerful symbolic meanings and energies that can greatly enhance the effectiveness of spells and rituals. As a direct gift from Mother Earth, herbs allow us to tap into the vital energies of the natural world, infusing our magical work with these potent forces.

Each herb carries its own set of symbolic associations and magical properties, which have been recognized and documented throughout history in various cultures. For example, lavender is widely acknowledged for its calming and peaceful properties, making it an excellent addition to spells focused on tranquility, healing, or love. Conversely, herbs like basil and cinnamon are revered for their associations with prosperity and success.

When incorporating herbs into spell work, their form and method of use can vary greatly. Some may be used fresh, while others might be dried. They can be burned as incense, added to charm bags, infused into oils or waters, or even used to dress candles for spells. The chosen method depends entirely on the spell and the intentions of the practitioner.

It's essential to source your herbs responsibly and understand the ethical considerations involved. Some herbs are endangered or harmful if used improperly. Therefore, proper research and understanding are key to their beneficial and responsible use.

In essence, herbs offer a practical, tangible way to connect with the natural energies of the Earth, enriching our spellcasting with their intrinsic qualities, making them an indispensable component of Wiccan practices.

Incense

Incense, with its richly aromatic smoke, is an integral part of many Wiccan rituals and spell work. The evocative swirls of fragrant smoke produced by incense serve multiple purposes, each deeply connected to the intentionality and focus that underpin all Wiccan practice.

The key role of incense lies in its ability to cleanse and consecrate a space, creating an atmosphere conducive to the work of magic. The smoke produced when incense is burned is believed to dispel negative energies, paving the way for positive vibrations. This act of purification prepares the practitioner and the space for the spell or ritual, marking a symbolic break from the mundane world.

The scent of the incense itself is very important. Various types of incense correspond with different intentions and magical properties. For instance, frankincense is often used for protection and spiritual growth, while sandalwood can aid in healing and meditation. Understanding these associations and selecting the appropriate incense can greatly enhance the effectiveness of your spells.

Furthermore, the act of burning incense can help to focus the mind and engage the senses, grounding the practitioner in the present moment. This sensory engagement can deepen one's connection to the spell work and strengthen its efficacy.

In essence, incense in Wicca serves as a powerful, sensory tool that enhances the magical environment, cleanses negative energy, and assists the practitioner in achieving a state of focused intent.

As we delve deeper into the use of these tools, it's important to note that they are just that - tools. They aren't inherently magical but are used to help focus your intention and energy. They are aids in your magical work, not the source of magic itself.

Safety precautions to consider while using these tools.

Safety is also an essential consideration when working with these tools. When working with candles, be aware of the risk of fire. Never leave a burning candle unattended and ensure you have a fire extinguisher accessible. With crystals and stones, be aware that some can be toxic or harmful if ingested or handled improperly. When using herbs, ensure you're aware of any potential allergic reactions or harmful effects they may have, particularly if you're using them in teas or other consumables.

We've laid the groundwork for understanding the role these tools play in Wiccan spellcasting and the importance of using them responsibly. Now let us delve into the details of how to use these tools effectively and safely in your spellcasting practice. The goal here is not to follow rigid rules, but rather to learn to adapt the tools to your personal practice and intentions.

Candles

Candles are frequently used in the Wiccan tradition to represent the God and Goddess, with a gold or yellow candle often representing the God and a silver or white candle representing the Goddess. The candle's flame also represents the transformative power of the divine. The act of lighting a candle is, in itself, a mini-ritual of change.

When engaging in spell work involving candles, understanding the materials and proper handling are paramount for both effectiveness and safety. Choosing the right type of candle is the first step. Beeswax or soy candles are generally preferred due to their natural origins, which align with Wicca's emphasis on nature. They also provide a cleaner burn, producing less soot and harmful fumes compared to paraffin-based candles, making them a safer choice for indoor use.

When using a candle in spell work, it's often a good practice to "dress" the candle. This involves anointing it with oils or carving symbols into it that align with your intention. As you prepare your candle in this way, focus on your goal, visualizing it clearly in your mind to charge the candle with your intent. Remember, though, when anointing a candle with oils, avoid getting oil on the wick as this could cause it to burn too quickly or unpredictably.

Candle safety is incredibly important. Always burn candles on a heat-resistant surface and away from any flammable materials. Keep them out of drafts to prevent uneven burning or flare-ups. Never leave a burning candle unattended and ensure it is completely extinguished when you are finished with your spell or ritual.

Lastly, consider the disposal of your candle remnants. If a spell calls for letting a candle burn down completely, ensure it is in a safe container that can handle the heat. If there are any remains left after the candle has served its purpose, dispose of them respectfully. Some practitioners choose to bury them in the earth, symbolizing the completion of the spell.

In essence, candle use in Wicca is a potent element that demands respect and care. When used safely and with clear intent, candles can illuminate your path towards manifesting your desires.

Crystals and Stones

The use of crystals and stones in spell work is a powerful way to tap into the energetic properties these natural elements possess. However, like all tools used in Wicca, it's important to handle and use them safely and respectfully.

When selecting a crystal or stone to use in your spell work, it's essential to take the time to connect with its unique energy. This can be done by holding it in your hand, closing your eyes, and opening yourself up to the sensations or thoughts it may inspire. Some people may feel a warmth or tingling sensation, or a sense of peace or clarity. It's a very personal experience and there's no right or wrong way to connect with a crystal.

Before using your crystals in spell work, it's recommended to cleanse them. This removes any residual energies they may have picked up. You can do this in several ways: bathing them in moonlight, burying them in the earth, rinsing them with purified water, or smudging them with sage. However, it's important to note that not all crystals can be cleansed with water as some are sensitive to it and may degrade, such as selenite and halite. Research or consult a knowledgeable source to determine the best method for your specific crystal or stone.

In your spells, you can incorporate crystals in various ways. They can be arranged on your altar to enhance the energy of your spell, placed in a spell jar as a physical representation of your intention, carried on your person as a constant energetic influence, or placed in a specific location that aligns with your intention. For instance, you might put a piece of rose quartz under your pillow to encourage loving dreams or place a protective black tourmaline near your front door.

Safety is also paramount when working with crystals and stones. Always handle them with care to avoid chipping or breaking them, as some crystals can have sharp edges that could cause injury. If you are creating a gem elixir or using crystals near water, make sure to verify that your chosen crystal is not toxic or water-soluble.

Remember, the goal of using crystals and stones in your spellwork is to harness their natural energies to aid in manifesting your intentions. Treating them with respect and care will help establish a positive energetic relationship, contributing to the effectiveness of your spells.

Herbs

Working with herbs in spellcasting is a practice rooted deep in history, adding a powerful element of the natural world to your magic. However, to ensure that you handle and use herbs safely and effectively, there are a few critical aspects to consider.

It's paramount to understand the properties of the herbs you're using. Many herbs have a rich array of associations in magical practice, corresponding to different intentions, deities, or elements. However, they also have physical properties that can affect your health. Some herbs may be toxic if ingested or come into contact with the skin, and others may have contraindications with certain medications or conditions. Always conduct thorough research or consult with a knowledgeable source before using a new herb in your spell work.

When you're ready to incorporate an herb into your spell, your method of application will depend on the purpose of your spell and the properties of the herb. If you're burning herbs, either directly or as part of an incense blend, it's vital to do so safely. Use a fire-safe dish or incense burner, and never leave burning herbs unattended. Some herbs can produce smoke that's irritating to the eyes or respiratory system, so ensure you're in a well-ventilated area and consider using a smaller amount of herb to start.

For spell jars or sachets, herbs can be mixed with other spell ingredients such as crystals, oils, or symbols written on paper. When working with dried herbs, be aware that they can sometimes be sharp and handle them carefully to avoid injury.

If you're incorporating herbs into a ritual bath, make sure that the herb is safe for topical application. Some herbs can cause skin irritation or allergic reactions. Always do a patch test first by applying a small amount of the herb (or a brew made from it) to a small area of your skin to check for any adverse reactions.

Remember that while herbs can add a potent element to your spells, their proper and respectful use is essential for safe and effective spellcasting. Always consider the physical and magical properties of the herbs you use, and let your intention guide you in their application. In this way, you can harness the vibrant power of the plant world to enhance your magical practice.

Incense

Incense holds a central role in many spiritual and magical practices. Its mystical smoke can clear negative energies, set the mood, and help manifest intentions into the universe. However, safety must always be considered when working with incense.

When selecting incense, aligning the scent with the intention of your spell can elevate your spell work. For instance, sage is known for its cleansing properties and is ideal for purifying a space or dispelling negative energy, while the soothing scent of lavender may aid in spells related to relaxation, peace, and emotional healing. This alignment not only enhances the potency of your spells but also helps create a more immersive and focused experience.

The safety measures regarding the use of incense are paramount. Always use a proper incense holder or burner. These holders are designed to contain the ash and keep the burning incense stable. If an incense stick or cone isn't secure, it could tip over and ignite nearby objects. If you're burning loose incense on charcoal, use a heat-resistant dish or censor. Always place your incense holder on a flat, stable surface away from flammable items such as curtains, papers, or combustible decor.

While incense creates an enchanting atmosphere, the smoke it produces should not be underestimated. Always ensure the area is well-ventilated, especially in small or enclosed spaces. Even natural incense smoke can be harmful if inhaled excessively or can exacerbate conditions such as asthma or allergies. Burning incense should be a sensory pleasure, not a discomfort or hazard.

A significant safety rule when using incense is never to leave it unattended. Incense may seem harmless due to its slow burn, but it is still a fire hazard. Always be present in the room where incense is burning, and make sure it's completely extinguished before leaving the room or going to bed.

Lastly, if you have pets or small children, make sure they can't reach the incense. Not only can the burning incense be a fire hazard, but small pieces can also be a choking hazard.

The respectful and safe use of incense can add a meaningful layer to your spellcasting, enhancing your sensory experience and creating a tangible connection between your intentions and the physical world.

These are just a few examples of how to use these tools in your spell work. As you continue your journey, you'll undoubtedly find new tools and methods that resonate with you. Just remember, the most powerful tool in any Wiccan's arsenal is their intention and focus. The physical tools are there to support and guide your energy, but the real magic comes from within you.

As we conclude this section, remember to handle all your tools and ingredients with respect and mindfulness. These items have their own energies, and when we use them in our spells, we are inviting their energies to mingle with ours. Use them wisely, and they can greatly enhance your magical workings. But also remember to be safe. Your magical practice should never put you or others in harm's way.

With the basic tools and safety precautions discussed, let's delve deeper into the world of spellcasting materials. Remember, these objects serve to focus your intent, and they aren't the sources of magic themselves. Always align your choices with your goals and personal beliefs for maximum effectiveness.

Altar Tools

The altar serves as a focal point for spellcasting and ritual work. Wiccan altar tools often include items like the athame (a ritual knife), chalice (a cup symbolizing the element of water), pentacle (a disc or plate with a pentagram inscribed on it), and wand. These tools align with the four cardinal elements and directions: the athame with air and the east, the wand with fire and the south, the chalice with water and the west, and the pentacle with earth and the north.

An athame, usually double-edged, is never used for physical cutting but symbolizes the power to make change. The wand, often made of wood, is used for directing energy. The chalice represents the Goddess and can hold water or wine during rituals. The pentacle, a five-pointed star within a circle, represents spirit dominating over the four elements and is often used as a tool of consecration.

Colors

Colors can be significant in Wiccan practices as they are believed to carry specific energies. Utilizing the correct colors in your spells can help align your intentions and enhance your spell's effectiveness. For example, you might use red for spells related to passion or courage, yellow for intellectual pursuits or communication, green for prosperity or growth, blue for healing and peace, and purple for spiritual growth or psychic abilities.

Symbols

Symbols are a powerful tool in spellcasting. They serve as physical representations of your intention and help focus your energy. Symbols can be drawn, engraved, or visualized during your spellcasting process. For instance, a heart symbol could be used in a love spell, while a dollar sign or rune of abundance might be used in a prosperity spell.

Oils and Essences

Oils and essences can be used in a variety of ways in Wiccan spellcasting. You might anoint candles with them, use them to dress your tools, add them to a ritual bath, or use them to create a particular atmosphere through scent. Like herbs, different oils and essences have different associations. Lavender oil, for example, might be used for peace and relaxation, while patchouli oil might be used for grounding and attracting prosperity.

Sacred Texts and Chants

Words hold power, and this is especially true in spellcasting. Sacred texts can be a source of inspiration and guidance, while chants, affirmations, or rhymes can serve to enhance your focus and solidify your intention. When creating your own spells, consider writing your own chant or affirmation that aligns closely with your specific intention.

Working with these tools and ingredients can significantly enhance your spellcasting experience and effectiveness. But remember, they are aids to help focus your intention and channel energy. They are not the source of power but are conduits to help you harness and direct the natural energies around and within you.

In the upcoming sections, we will discuss more about the various aspects of spells and the significance of the Wiccan calendar in spell-casting. This will further help you understand the broader context in which spells are cast, making your practice more meaningful and effective. It's a fascinating journey that requires patience, respect for nature and its forces, and a commitment to personal growth and learning. So let's continue with this journey together.

Conclusion

Now, having traversed through the varied world of spellcasting tools and ingredients, we can see that each object has its own unique role to play. From candles to crystals, herbs to incense, altar tools to symbolic colors, each element is a strand in the intricate web of Wiccan spellcasting. These tools serve as a bridge, helping us focus our intentions, harness energies, and connect with the divine.

Remember, the tools you select should align with your personal beliefs and intentions. Just as each of us has a unique fingerprint, our magical practices will be uniquely our own. What works for one person might not work for another, and that's okay. Trust your instincts and intuition, for they are your best guides in this journey.

It's important to note that while these tools are powerful aids, the real magic comes from within you. These are conduits to help you harness and focus your innate power and the natural energies around you. Your intent, focus, and will are at the core of every spell.

Safety is a crucial aspect to consider. As you've learned, each tool comes with its safety precautions. Always research, understand, and respect the tools and ingredients you work with. Your spellcasting practice should be a space of comfort, growth, and safety.

Finally, remember that the acquisition of tools shouldn't become a barrier to your practice. You don't need to have every tool to begin. Start with what you have, and gradually add to your toolset as you grow in your practice. The Wiccan path is one of respect - for self, for others, and for the natural world. Let this respect guide your interactions with your tools, just as it guides your actions in life.

As we close this chapter, remember that you are embarking on a journey of discovery and growth. In Wicca, learning is a spiral, not a straight line. You'll circle back to concepts again and again, each time with a deeper understanding. This chapter on tools and ingredients for spells is just one loop in that spiral. Embrace the journey with an open mind and heart, and you'll find the path unfolds before you in beautiful, unexpected ways. Until the next chapter, blessed be.

The Wiccan Calendar and Its Significance

I n our exploration of Wicca and its practices, we've discovered the importance of nature in Wiccan beliefs, the significance of tools in spellcasting, and now, we'll turn our focus to time. More specifically, the way Wiccans mark time through a sacred calendar known as the Wheel of the Year. Understanding this calendar and its significance is vital for anyone delving into Wicca and its spellcasting traditions.

The Wheel of the Year is a cycle that symbolizes the eternal rhythm of life, death, and rebirth. The calendar isn't merely a way to track days, months, and seasons. It's a spiritual tool that Wiccans use to attune themselves with natural rhythms and cycles, reminding us of our connection with nature and the divine.

The Wiccan calendar is a circle, a wheel, reflecting the cyclical nature of life. It comprises eight festivals or Sabbats that mark the changing seasons and the journey of the Sun God throughout the year.

These Sabbats are a combination of Celtic and Norse pagan festivals, as well as agricultural celebrations that have been observed by various cultures throughout history.

As we embark on this exploration of the Wheel of the Year, we'll learn about each Sabbat, its significance, and the ways they can influence our spellcasting. We'll also discuss the importance of Esbats, which are celebrations of the moon phases, another crucial aspect of the Wiccan calendar.

Let's begin our journey with the overview of the eight Sabbats:

- **Yule (Winter Solstice)**: Typically celebrated on December 21st, Yule marks the shortest day of the year. It's a celebration of the rebirth of the Sun God, symbolizing hope and new beginnings. Despite the cold and darkness, Yule reminds us that light will return.

- **Imbolc**: Celebrated on February 1st or 2nd, Imbolc signifies the awakening of the earth as winter begins to thaw. It's a time to celebrate the first signs of spring and the return of the light.

- **Ostara (Spring Equinox)**: Usually falling on March 21st, Ostara is a celebration of balance and renewal. Day and night are of equal length, and the earth is coming alive with new growth.

- **Beltane**: Celebrated on May 1st, Beltane marks the height of spring and the start of summer. It's a time of fertility and abundance.

- **Litha (Summer Solstice)**: Usually celebrated on June 21st, Litha marks the longest day of the year. It's a celebration of the Sun God in his full power.

- **Lughnasadh**: Celebrated on August 1st, Lughnasadh is the start of the harvest season. It's a time to begin reaping what we have sown, both literally and metaphorically.

- **Mabon (Autumn Equinox)**: Falling around September 21st, Mabon is a time of balance, just like Ostara. However, at Mabon, we are moving from light into darkness as the days start to shorten.

- **Samhain**: Celebrated on October 31st, Samhain is considered the Wiccan New Year. It's a time to honor our ancestors, celebrate the harvest, and prepare for the dark half of the year.

Sabbats are an essential component of Wicca, each offering an opportunity to reflect, honor the divine, and align ourselves with the natural rhythm of the Earth. The Sabbats do not merely represent the changing seasons, but they also symbolize the cycles of life, death, and rebirth, as well as the eternal dance between the God and the Goddess.

Now that we have a broad understanding of the Sabbats let's delve deeper into their meanings, significance, and how they can guide and enhance our spellcasting practices.

Imbolc, observed on February 1st, is an important waypoint on the Wiccan Wheel of the Year, marking the midpoint between the Winter Solstice (Yule) and the Spring Equinox (Ostara). This period is one of great anticipation, as the initial signs of spring start to break through the frosty veneer of winter. It is a time of swelling potential and the promise of renewal.

The Goddess, in her transformative journey, emerges in her maiden guise, an embodiment of freshness, vitality, and boundless possibilities. Simultaneously, the God, synchronizing with the solar cycle, is gradually gaining strength, an event mirrored by the steadily lengthening days.

Wiccans recognize this transition phase as an optimal time for purification rituals, casting off the worn and obsolete to pave the way for new beginnings. As such, Imbolc is often marked with thorough physical and spiritual cleanings, an exercise in clearing out old energies to make room for the new.

Moreover, Imbolc holds great significance in the realm of spellcasting. Spells woven during this time bear the vigorous energy of renewal. As such, spells for personal growth, self-improvement, healing, and inspiration, those that embrace the essence of fresh starts, are particularly potent when cast during the Imbolc season. The rejuvenating energy of Imbolc, therefore, provides a potent backdrop for transformative magic, further enhancing the spellcaster's intent and focus.

Beltane, traditionally celebrated on the first day of May, is a vibrant festival on the Wiccan Wheel of the Year, signifying the arrival of summer and the rich fertility of the earth. The Goddess, at this time, fully embodies her mother aspect, resplendent in her radiant glory. The God, equally powerful, engages with the Goddess in a sacred union, a mystical marriage that results in the bounty of life, bringing forth abundance and growth in nature.

Fire, a symbol of purification and transformation, holds significant importance during Beltane. Towering Beltane fires are lit, serving as beacons that ward off malevolent spirits, and as catalysts for transformation. Some Wiccans uphold the tradition of "jumping the Beltane fire," an act symbolizing purification and the intention to manifest growth in the upcoming season.

Beltane's energy aligns exceptionally well with certain types of spells. The festival's emphasis on fertility and prosperity makes it a perfect time for casting spells for love, abundance, and growth. Whether you're seeking to kindle a new romance, fortify an existing relationship, enhance fertility, or increase prosperity, Beltane is an opportune moment to perform such spell work. The jubilant, passionate energy of this time magnifies the potency of spells, aligning your intent with the flourishing life force of the season.

Lughnasadh, also referred to as Lammas, occurs around the beginning of August and is a crucial milestone on the Wiccan Wheel of the Year, marking the commencement of the harvest season. This significant celebration is the first of the three harvest festivals—Lughnasadh, Mabon, and Samhain.

At this time of year, the fruits of labor are ready to be harvested, both in the literal sense with crops ripening in the fields, and metaphorically in our personal lives. We start to see the results of the efforts we've expended and the seeds we've sown in previous months. It's a period of recognition and reflection, as well as an opportunity to make adjustments for the remaining harvest season.

Simultaneously, this period symbolizes the beginning of the decline of the God's power. Even as the earth reaches the peak of its productivity, the God's strength begins to wane, signaling the impending arrival of the darker half of the year.

The themes of Lughnasadh revolve around gratitude and acknowledgment of our blessings. It's a time to offer thanks for the abundance in our lives and to share our bounty with others. This energy of abundance, gratitude, and success makes it an appropriate time for corresponding spells. Casting spells to attract success, to express gratitude, and to enhance abundance in all areas of life can be particularly potent and effective during the season of Lughnasadh.

Samhain, typically celebrated at the end of October, is often perceived as the most potent and sacred of all the Sabbats in the Wiccan calendar. This date marks the end of the harvest season and the onset of the darker half of the year, a time symbolizing death and the beginning of a spiritual new year. It's a moment of profound reflection, endings, and new beginnings.

During Samhain, the veil separating our world from the spirit realm is considered to be at its thinnest, providing enhanced opportunities for communication with the spirits, ancestors, and the divine. This heightened connectivity can lead to more profound insights, more vivid dreams, and an enhanced sense of intuition.

Samhain is a time of remembrance and honoring those who have passed. Rituals often include elements of ancestor veneration, such as creating altars in their honor or holding a feast to celebrate their lives. Simultaneously, this Sabbat encourages introspection, offering an opportunity to seek guidance for the future and contemplate the cycle of life, death, and rebirth.

Given the nature of Samhain, spells and rituals focusing on protection, divination, and spirit communication are particularly potent. This period is ideal for practicing divination methods such as tarot reading or scrying to seek insights for the coming year. Casting spells for protection is also fitting, as it can provide a spiritual barrier against any negative or harmful energies that may be more accessible during this time. Finally, rites or spells that facilitate communication with spirits can be especially powerful and effective during the sacred time of Samhain.

Interwoven with the Sabbats in the Wiccan calendar are the Esbats, rituals or celebrations that take place in alignment with the phases of the moon. The Esbats are lunar observances, offering a counterbalance to the solar festivals represented by the Sabbats, which follow the journey of the Sun God throughout the year.

The Esbats specifically honor the Goddess, celebrated in her three aspects: maiden, mother, and crone. These aspects mirror the phases of the moon – waxing, full, and waning, respectively – each representing a different stage of the Goddess's life cycle, as well as the cycle of life itself.

The most notable Esbat is the Full Moon ritual, a time of high energy and power when magic is at its most potent. It's a time for casting spells, making amulets, and performing significant rites. The New Moon, on the other hand, signifies new beginnings, making it an excellent time for initiating new projects and intentions.

The Dark Moon, or the time when the moon isn't visible in the sky, is often associated with the crone aspect of the Goddess. It's a period for introspection, rest, and shadow work, providing the chance to delve into the deeper, darker parts of oneself and confront hidden fears or issues.

Esbats are occasions for individual Wiccans and covens to gather, perform magic, honor the Goddess, and attune themselves to the moon's cycles. They are a testament to the importance of the moon and the Goddess in Wicca and serve as a reminder of the harmonious balance between the feminine and masculine divine.

Esbats occur every full moon, new moon, and for some practitioners, during the waxing and waning moons as well. The full moon Esbats are times of great power and are ideal for divination, banishing, and protection spells, while the new moon is a time for new beginnings, growth, and healing spells.

Understanding and aligning with the Wiccan calendar can significantly enhance your spellcasting. By attuning with the natural rhythms, you're not just casting spells, but harmonizing your intentions with the universal energies. This can empower your spells and bring you closer to achieving your spiritual goals.

Now, having understood the concept of Sabbats and Esbats, let's delve deeper into the significance of moon phases in spellcasting in the remaining section of this chapter. As the moon waxes and wanes, it offers different energies that can be harnessed to amplify our spells, making this celestial body an essential part of Wiccan rituals.

Let's delve deeper into understanding the Moon, its phases, and the effect each phase can have on our spellcasting and rituals.

The Moon, in all its phases, has been a guiding light for witches and practitioners for centuries. Its ebb and flow are a visual and symbolic representation of the cycle of death and rebirth, of transformation and change. This lunar cycle can be harnessed to give our spells and rituals more potency.

In Wicca, the Moon isn't just a physical entity in the sky; it's a symbol of the divine feminine and is often associated with the Goddess. Its changing phases reflect the different aspects of the Goddess - maiden, mother, and crone.

The New Moon, also known as the Dark Moon, signifies beginnings and is a time of rebirth and creation. It's the ideal time to plant the seeds of your intentions, to start new projects, or to breathe life into new ideas. During this phase, spells for new beginnings, growth, and creativity are particularly effective.

As the Moon starts to wax, or increase in size, it symbolizes growth and attraction. This is the phase where you want to focus on spells that draw things to you, be it love, prosperity, success, or healing.

The Full Moon is a time of heightened energy and power. It's when the moon is at its peak and its influence is strongest. This is an excellent time for divination, for spells that require a lot of energy, or for any spell that you want to give an extra power boost. It's also a time of fulfillment and realization, making it ideal for rituals that celebrate achievements and personal growth.

As the Moon begins to wane, or decrease in size, it moves into a phase of release and letting go. This is the perfect time for banishing spells, for breaking bad habits, or for releasing anything that no longer serves you.

Lastly, there's the Dark Moon, the period just before the moon starts its new cycle. This phase is a time for deep introspection, for rest, and for honoring the darkness before the light returns. It's a time for soul-searching, for divination that seeks deep wisdom, and for spells that deal with endings.

Understanding these phases, and planning your spells accordingly, can make a significant difference in your spell work. It's a way to harness the natural energies of the earth and sky, to align your intentions with the universe, and to draw upon the Goddess's power in her many forms.

As we continue our journey into Wicca and spellcasting, remember that it's not just about the spells themselves. It's about the connection we forge with the world around us, the respect and reverence we have for nature and the divine, and the personal transformation we undergo in the process. As you learn to navigate the Wiccan calendar and the phases of the moon, you'll discover that every day holds the potential for magic, every moment is ripe with the possibility of transformation, and every spell is an opportunity to touch the divine.

In the end, it's about finding your own rhythm, honoring your own path, and embracing the power within you. As you align yourself with the cycles of the Wheel of the Year and the phases of the moon, you'll not only become a more effective spellcaster, but you'll also deepen your connection with the natural world and, by extension, the divine.

Remember, the Wheel of the Year and its moon cycles are not just dates on a calendar but a spiritual roadmap guiding you through a never-ending journey of self-discovery, growth, and transformation.

You are not a mere bystander in the dance of the universe, but an active participant. By syncing your life with these natural cycles, you start to flow with the rhythm of the universe rather than against it. You'll find that your actions are more effortless, your spells more potent, and your spiritual life more fulfilling.

Now, let's take a step back and look at the bigger picture. What does it mean to be a part of this grand cycle, this Wheel of the Year? It's about understanding that we are all a part of a greater whole. Each of us, like the festivals and the moon phases, plays a vital part in the grand tapestry of life. We are interconnected with nature and with each other.

By observing the Sabbats, we're not just honoring the changing seasons, but we're also recognizing and honoring the changes within ourselves. By paying attention to the moon phases, we're aligning ourselves with its ebb and flow, and in doing so, learning to embrace our own cycles of change and growth. The Wheel of the Year is not just a measure of time, but a mirror reflecting our own journey.

The energy of the universe doesn't just flow around us; it flows through us. By learning how to harness this energy - through spell-casting, observing the Sabbats and moon phases, or any other form of spiritual practice - we become conduits of this divine power.

In Wicca, every action is imbued with intention, every moment is magical, and every breath is a prayer. We honor the divine in all its forms and in all its manifestations - in the change of seasons, in the moon's glow, in the elements around us, and in the depths of our souls.

As you walk this path, remember that the journey itself is the destination. There will always be more to learn, more to experience, and more to discover about the universe and about yourself. Embrace the journey with an open heart and an open mind, and the Wheel of the Year will always guide you home.

As we conclude this chapter, take a moment to reflect on what you've learned and how it applies to your own journey. The Wiccan calendar is not just about days and dates; it's about a way of life. By understanding and embracing the Wheel of the Year and the phases of the moon, you're taking an important step in your spiritual journey.

As you turn the wheel, may you find wisdom in the changing seasons, strength in the moon's glow, and magic in every moment. Blessed be.

Casting Your First Spells

A s we turn the page to Chapter 5, it's time to get practical and start with the basics of spell casting. We've spent a good amount of time understanding the philosophy and principles of Wicca, now let's put that knowledge into practice.

Before we dive into the art of casting spells, there are some vital preparatory steps to discuss. These preparations not only help enhance the efficacy of your spells but also ensure you carry out your magical work in a safe and protected environment.

Casting Your First Spells

- Firstly, let's delve into the fundamental concept of grounding. Grounding is an essential practice within Wiccan rituals and spellcasting, facilitating a deep connection between your energy and that of the Earth. It can be likened to an electrical circuit – just as a physical wire grounds electrical charge to prevent overloads, grounding in a spiritual sense balances your energy and averts any potential energetic overwhelm.

- Grounding is exceptionally beneficial both prior to and after conducting spell work. It serves to clear your mind, stabilizing your energetic frequency, which ultimately enhances your focus. Not only does it improve concentration, but it also aids in managing and releasing emotional tension, fostering a sense of peace and tranquility.

- So, how exactly do you ground yourself? Below is a simplified technique that anyone, from beginners to advanced practitioners, can employ:

- 1. Choose a comfortable position, either sitting or standing, ensuring your feet are touching the ground. Take a moment to feel the solid connection between you and the Earth.

- 2. Close your eyes and begin taking deep, calming breaths, allowing your body to relax and your mind to quieten.

- 3. In your mind's eye, visualize a sturdy root or a cord extending from the base of your spine or from the soles of your feet, reaching deep into the heart of the Earth.

- 4. As you continue to breathe deeply, imagine the stabilizing energy of the Earth ascending up this root or cord, filling your body with a calming, grounding energy. This energy is warm, comforting, and firm, reminding you of your connection to the world around you.

- 5. Concurrently, envision any surplus or negative energy being drawn down into the Earth through this connection, where it is neutralized and harmlessly dispersed. This could be visualized as a dark smoke or cloud, which lightens and dissipates as it moves down the cord and into the Earth.

- 6. Take a few more deep, cleansing breaths, each exhale further anchoring you to the Earth. When you feel centered and connected, gently open your eyes.

- This grounding practice is a cornerstone of Wiccan spellcasting, cultivating a balance that empowers the practitioner to wield their energy effectively and responsibly.

- Centering, as a companion practice to grounding, is another crucial aspect of spellcasting preparation. While grounding is about forming a connection with Earth's energy, centering is the practice of aligning your personal energy, essentially creating a 'center' within you. This involves drawing your consciousness into the present moment, finding your inner balance, and preparing yourself to channel energy effectively and mindfully.

- Centering is a process of self-awareness, directing attention inward, and creating a sense of equilibrium. It enables the harmonization of your thoughts, emotions, and physical sensations, which subsequently promotes clarity and focus. Centering is particularly essential when spellcasting as it assists you in commanding your personal energy, essential for intention setting and manifestation.

- Here is a method to center yourself:

- 1. Adopt a comfortable seated position, your feet maintaining contact with the ground. Close your eyes, letting your body relax as you start to take deep, conscious breaths, pushing aside any distracting thoughts.

- 2. Now, visualize your personal energy. Imagine it as a radiant ball of light located at your core, around your solar plexus area. This effulgent light symbolizes your personal power, your consciousness, the essence of your being.

- 3. As you continue to breathe deeply, envision this luminous energy ball growing increasingly brighter and more stable. Picture it as a beacon, aligning your physical, emotional, and spiritual aspects, harmonizing them into a balanced whole.

- 4. Remain in this visualization for a few moments, allowing yourself to immerse in the tranquility and stability it imparts. You might feel a sense of peace, balance, and focused attention—signs of effective centering.

- 5. When you feel ready and your energy feels aligned and balanced, gradually open your eyes, carrying this centered state into your spellcasting.

- Remember, just like grounding, centering is a vital step to effective and balanced spell work. It helps you command your personal energy, ultimately empowering your spellcasting abilities.

Grounding and centering are essential not just in spellcasting but in any magical work. They help you to focus your energy, maintain your balance, and prepare you physically, emotionally, and spiritually for the work at hand.

But before we start casting spells, there's one more thing we need to cover: the casting of a protective circle.

Guide to casting a protective circle.

Casting Your First Spells

- Once you have effectively grounded and centered your energy, the next essential step in your spellcasting process is casting a protective circle. This practice extends beyond the realm of practical magic, serving a pivotal role in creating a sacred, undisturbed space for your ritualistic work.

- Casting a protective circle forms an energetic boundary against unwanted external influences and energies. Think of it as a personalized sanctuary, an intimate haven where only the energies you intentionally summon can permeate. This invisible circle also helps contain and concentrate the energies you raise during your spell work, making your ritual more potent.

- Here's a detailed approach to casting a protective circle:

- 1. Identify the space where you will perform your spell. Make yourself comfortable, either standing or sitting, within this area. Close your eyes and engage in a few rounds of deep, rhythmic breathing to center yourself.

- 2. Begin in the northern direction, letting a vivid image form in your mind: a radiant white or blue light, radiating from your hand or wand. Moving clockwise around your space, visualize this light sketching a circular boundary. Envision it extending both above and below you, encapsulating you within a protective, energetic sphere.

- 3. During the process of casting, you might choose to invoke the elements (Earth, Air, Fire, Water) or deities for added protection. An invocation could be as simple as saying, "I cast this circle of light to safeguard me during this rite. May it shield me from any negativity or harm."

- 4. After completing the circle, pause and acutely feel the energy within your sacred space. It should exude a sense of calm, security, and distinctly differ from the energy outside the circle.

- To close the circle post-spell, reverse your casting steps. Initiate again from the north, but this time, move counterclockwise. Visualize the radiant light you cast earlier, gradually receding and returning to you as you trace your path. Extend your gratitude to the elements or deities you invoked, acknowledging their protection. Conclude with a definitive statement like, "The circle is open, yet remains unbroken."

- Remember, the protective circle is not a physical boundary but a psychological and energetic one, a cornerstone for a secure, effective, and focused spellcasting experience.

N ow, you're ready to begin spellcasting. Let's start with a few simple spells that are perfect for beginners. Remember, the purpose of these initial spells is to familiarize you with the process. Don't be discouraged if you don't see immediate results. Like any skill, effective spellcasting takes time and practice. But trust in the process, and trust in your own power.

As we proceed, remember the three P's of spellcasting: preparation, precision, and patience. Preparation involves grounding, centering, and casting your circle, as we just discussed. Precision refers to clearly focusing your intentions and closely following the spell instructions. And patience... well, the universe often works in its own time, so don't be disheartened if your spells don't yield instant results. It's about the journey, remember?

Now, let's walk this path together as we cast your first spells.

Let's begin our spellcasting journey with a simple yet powerful spell for clarity and focus. This spell will help clear your mind and bring about a sense of focus and calmness. Here are the step-by-step instructions:

Spell for Clarity and Focus

You'll need: A clear quartz crystal, a white candle, and a quiet space.

- Begin by grounding and centering yourself. Once you feel calm and centered, cast your protective circle.

- Light the white candle. As you do so, envision the flame burning away any confusion or distracting thoughts.

- Hold the clear quartz in your hands. Quartz is a powerful crystal known for its clarity-enhancing properties. As you hold the crystal, visualize its energy merging with your own, imbuing you with clear thoughts and sharp focus.

- Say the following words (or similar, if you prefer): "With clear mind and focused intent, I banish confusion and discontent. In its place, may clarity flow, guiding me in the paths I go."

- Sit quietly for a few moments, focusing on the energy of the candle and the crystal. When you feel ready, thank the elements and deities (if any were invoked), extinguish the candle, and close the circle.

- Carry the crystal with you, especially during times when you need extra focus or clarity.

This is just one example of a simple spell that beginners can perform. As you can see, it involves clear intention, specific tools, and a process that combines these elements to create change.

Take time to practice this spell and others like it. Notice how the process makes you feel. Do you feel empowered? More connected to the natural world? This sense of connection and empowerment is a significant part of spellcasting.

Remember, while the specific tools and words can lend power to your spells, the most important ingredient is your intention. Believe in your ability to create change, trust in the power of your intent, and know that with every spell you cast, you are becoming more attuned to the magic that exists all around you.

In the following chapters, we will explore more specific spells designed to foster love, attract prosperity, promote healing, and protect against negativity. But for now, practice with these basics. Your journey into the world of Wicca is just beginning, and there's so much more to discover!

It's worth reflecting on how far you've come in your journey into Wicca and spellcasting. You've not only learned about grounding and centering, but you've also learned how to create a protective circle, and even cast your very first spell. This is no small feat. In these practices, you've taken your first steps into an enchanting world that harmonizes with the natural energies that exist all around us.

Casting your first spell is a significant milestone in any witch's journey. It represents a willingness to step into your power and an openness to a universe that pulses with energy and possibility. Whether you were casting along with the spell for clarity and focus, or whether you were simply reading and learning, give yourself a moment to recognize and celebrate this achievement.

Remember, the spellcasting process isn't solely about the results. Sure, it's exciting to see your intentions manifest in the physical world, but don't get too caught up in the end goal. The true beauty of spellcasting is found in the process: the quiet moment of grounding, the tangible act of creating a sacred space, the whisper of intention set out into the universe. This process aligns you with the energies of the universe and helps you recognize your own innate power.

And yet, even as we celebrate these first steps, it's essential to remember that this is just the beginning of your journey. You've dipped your toes into the vast ocean of spellcasting, but there's still so much more to explore and understand. Over time, you'll learn to work with different tools, cast more complex spells, and even write your own spells, custom-made for your unique intentions and desires.

As you move forward in your journey, I encourage you to approach your practice with a sense of curiosity and wonder. This is your opportunity to connect with the universe on a deeper level, to tap into the ancient wisdom of Wicca, and to truly harness the power that lies within you. It's an exciting journey, full of potential and brimming with magic.

Remember to be patient with yourself. Spellcasting, like any other skill, takes time and practice to master. Even experienced witches continue to learn and grow in their craft. Every spell you cast, every ritual you perform, is another step on your unique path. Trust the process and know that every step, every stumble, every moment of wonder, is part of your journey.

In the end, whether you're casting spells for love, prosperity, protection, or personal growth, the practice of spellcasting is a powerful tool for transformation. By harnessing the natural energies that surround us, you can manifest changes in your life and align yourself more closely with your truest self.

This is the magic of Wicca, the magic of spellcasting, and now, it's your magic. Hold onto this feeling as you move forward, through the challenges, the triumphs, and everything in between. Embrace the journey, and let your magic shine. After all, you're a spellcaster now.

Bonus Spell For Beginners

A Simple Spell for Tranquility and Peace

You'll need: A blue candle, lavender oil, a small piece of paper, a pen, and a quiet space.

- Preparation: Begin by finding a quiet and comfortable place where you won't be disturbed. Take a few moments to ground and center yourself, letting go of any stress or worries from the day.

- Creating a Sacred Space: As with our previous spells, it's essential to create a sacred space by casting a protective circle. Envision a sphere of glowing light around you, creating a boundary that will keep you safe and hold your intentions during your spellcasting.

- Setting up the Spell: Take the blue candle (which represents tranquility and peace) and place it before you. Anoint the candle with the lavender oil, starting at the middle and moving towards the ends. As you do so, envision peace and calm flowing into the candle.

- Writing your Intentions: On the piece of paper, write down what you seek tranquility from. This could be a specific situation causing you stress, or it could be a more general wish for peace and calm in your life. Fold the paper and place it under the candle.

- Casting the Spell: Light the candle. As you do, say the following (or similar words that resonate with you): "Tranquility flow, peace be still, calmness I summon, by my will."

- Meditation: Sit quietly for a few moments, watching the candle's flame. Visualize the flame's calming blue energy spreading out and enveloping you, washing away any anxieties or concerns, and replacing them with a deep sense of peace and tranquility.

- Ending the Spell: When you feel ready, say a word of thanks to the elements and any deities you might have invoked. Then, snuff out the candle and release the circle, envisioning the sphere of light fading, leaving you grounded in your space, but carrying with you the tranquility and peace from your spell. Keep the piece of paper somewhere safe or dispose of it in a respectful way, like burning or burying it.

- Remember: This spell can be repeated whenever you need a little extra peace in your life. You may find that with practice, the sense of tranquility it brings becomes stronger and more immediate.

Spellcasting is a personal journey, and each spell you cast is an opportunity to connect with the natural world, your deities, and your own inner wisdom. Embrace these connections, and remember that every spell you cast brings you one step closer to the divine energies that make up our universe. Happy spellcasting!

Spells for Love and Relationships

L ove, one of the most profound human emotions, has a central place in many magical traditions, including Wicca. It's no surprise, then, that spells related to love and relationships are among the most commonly sought out. This chapter will delve into those magical practices that can help foster self-love, strengthen existing relationships, and attract new love into your life.

But before we begin, it's crucial to touch on the topic of ethics, especially when it comes to love spells. When it comes to love and relationships, the intentions behind our magical workings need to be as pure and unselfish as possible. That means respecting free will – not only yours but others' as well. To try and influence another's feelings or actions against their will is not just unethical, but it also goes against the core tenets of Wicca.

As Wiccans, we follow the Wiccan Rede, "An' it harm none, do what ye will." This rule is especially relevant when working with love spells. Love spells should never be about controlling or manipulating others. They should be about opening your heart to love, enhancing the love already present, healing from past hurt, or attracting a compatible partner while allowing for their free will.

Remember that our magic, and love magic in particular, should not seek to infringe upon anyone's free will or cause harm. Consider love spells as ways of sending out a call to the universe about what you desire in a respectful and consensual way. Like a message in a bottle cast out to sea, it's about expressing your heart's desire, not about dictating the response that you get.

Furthermore, it's also essential to recognize the importance of working on the mundane level in conjunction with your spells. Magic can give us a nudge in the right direction, but it can't replace the need for open communication, mutual respect, and effort in a relationship. Love spells are most effective when they are supplemented by the real-world work we do to foster and maintain our relationships.

So, as we explore the realm of love spells, remember to use them responsibly, ethically, and in harmony with the free will of others. Now, with that foundation laid, let's move forward and explore some specific spells for self-love, strengthening relationships, and attracting love.

Now that we've laid the groundwork for self-love, let's move on to how we can use Wiccan spells to enhance our relationships with others. Remember, the goal here is not to manipulate or coerce others. Instead, we're looking to foster genuine connections, enhance existing relationships, and attract the kind of love that is right for us.

- Spell for Strengthening a Relationship: Relationships, whether romantic, platonic, or familial, can all benefit from a little magical boost. This spell uses the energy of unity and growth to strengthen the bond between two people. It can be used to deepen a connection, improve communication, or heal minor misunderstandings.

- Spell for Attracting Love: This spell isn't about making a specific person fall in love with you. Rather, it's about opening your life to the possibility of love, making yourself more receptive to it, and attracting a love that's right for you. It's an excellent spell for those who are single and ready to welcome a new relationship.

- Spell for Harmony in Relationships: Sometimes, relationships go through rocky patches where the energy between the involved parties feels off, and misunderstandings seem to pile up. This spell works to restore harmony and balance, bringing back the peaceful, loving energy that should be present in a loving relationship.

These spells should be tailored to your needs and circumstances. Feel free to modify the ingredients, chants, or any part of the spell that doesn't resonate with you. Remember, your intention and the energy you put into the spell are what truly matters. Now, let's get into the specifics of these love and relationship spells.

Spell for Fostering Self-Love

You'll need: A rose quartz crystal, a pink candle, a piece of paper, a pen, and a quiet space.

- Preparation: Begin by finding a quiet, comfortable space where you won't be disturbed. Take a few moments to ground and center yourself, focusing on the present moment and letting go of any external worries or thoughts.

- Creating a Sacred Space: Cast a protective circle around your space, imagining a sphere of glowing light around you that will protect and contain your intentions during your spell-casting.

- Setting Up the Spell: Place the pink candle (representing love) in front of you, and place the rose quartz (a stone associated with self-love and emotional healing) next to it.

- Writing Your Intentions: On the piece of paper, write down positive affirmations of self-love. These could be things you love about yourself, things you're proud of, or aspects you're working on loving more. Phrases could be like, "I am worthy of love," or, "I love and accept myself unconditionally."

- Casting the Spell: Light the candle and say the following words or any that resonate with your intent: "With this light, I ignite self-love. As I shine, so does my love from within."

- Meditation: Holding the rose quartz, read aloud or silently meditate on the affirmations you wrote down. Visualize each affirmation filling you up with a warm, pink light, growing with every word.

- Ending the Spell: After you've gone through all your affirmations, sit quietly for a few moments, basking in the feelings of self-love. When you're ready, say a word of thanks for this self-love. Then, snuff out the candle and release the circle, visualizing the protective light dissipating, leaving you grounded but still filled with the love from your spell.

- Follow-Up: Keep the piece of paper with your affirmations and the rose quartz somewhere you'll see them often as a reminder of your inherent self-love. This spell can be repeated as needed, and over time, you should find your feelings of self-love strengthening.

Remember, spellcasting is a deeply personal experience, and you're encouraged to modify this spell to better fit your path and preferences. You deserve love, especially from yourself, so don't shy away from performing this spell as many times as needed. Remember, the most potent magic starts from within.

Spell for Strengthening a Relationship

You'll need: Two pink candles, a piece of paper, a pen, a piece of rose quartz, and a quiet space.

- Preparation: As always, begin by finding a quiet, comfortable space where you won't be disturbed. Ground and center yourself, focusing on your present intentions and the person you wish to strengthen your bond with.

- Creating a Sacred Space: Cast a protective circle around your space, envisioning a sphere of protective light that will contain your intentions during your spellcasting.

- Setting Up the Spell: Position the two pink candles (representing the two individuals in the relationship) side by side, and place the rose quartz (a stone associated with love) between them.

- Writing Your Intentions: On the piece of paper, write down your heartfelt intentions for the relationship. These could include wishes for better communication, deeper understanding, more patience, shared growth, etc. Be as specific and sincere as possible.

- Casting the Spell: Light the candles and say the following words or any that resonate with your intent: "With this light, I ignite a stronger bond, a deeper understanding, and an ever-growing love between us."

- Meditation: Hold the rose quartz and read aloud or silently meditate on the intentions you wrote down. Visualize these intentions being absorbed by the rose quartz and then radiating out to envelop the candles and, symbolically, the relationship you're focusing on.

- Ending the Spell: After you've gone through all your intentions, sit quietly for a few moments, basking in the feelings of love and connection. When you're ready, express gratitude for the love and unity you share. Snuff out the candles and release the circle, visualizing the protective light dissipating, but leaving the strengthened bond between you and the other person.

- Follow-Up: Keep the piece of paper with your intentions and the rose quartz somewhere you'll see them often, like your bedroom or living area. This spell can be repeated whenever you feel the need to reinforce your bond further.

Always remember that communication is key in any relationship. This spell is a spiritual aid and should be used alongside open, honest dialogue and mutual respect. Let the enhanced connection be felt not just in the spell, but in your everyday interactions as well.

Spell for Attracting Love

You'll need: A rose or pink candle, a piece of paper, a red pen, dried rose petals, and a small pouch or cloth bag.

- Preparation: Begin by finding a quiet, comfortable space where you won't be disturbed. As always, ground and center yourself, focusing on your desire to attract love into your life.

- Creating a Sacred Space: Cast a protective circle around your space, visualizing a sphere of protective energy that will contain your intentions during your spellcasting.

- Setting Up the Spell: Position the rose or pink candle (representing love) in front of you.

- Writing Your Intentions: On the piece of paper, write down your intentions for your future love. You could include traits you desire in a partner, how you want to feel in the relationship, or specific wishes for your romantic life. Be honest and specific.

- Casting the Spell: Light the candle and say the following words or any that resonate with your intent: "By the power of this flame, I open my heart and life to the love that is waiting for me."

- Meditation: Read aloud or silently meditate on the intentions you wrote down. Visualize these intentions rising with the smoke of the candle and being sent out into the universe.

- Creating a Love Talisman: Place the paper with your intentions and some rose petals into the small pouch or cloth bag. This becomes a talisman—a physical representation of your intentions to attract love.

- Ending the Spell: After you've spent some time meditating on your intentions, thank the universe for listening and express gratitude for the love that is on its way to you. Snuff out the candle and release the circle, visualizing the protective energy dissipating, but your intentions remaining strong.

- Follow-Up: Keep the talisman somewhere personal to you, like under your pillow or in your purse. Its presence serves as a constant reminder of your intentions and a beacon for attracting love.

Remember, this spell isn't about making a specific person fall in love with you. It's about opening yourself to the possibility of love and attracting a love that's right for you. Patience and positivity are key as you wait for your intentions to manifest.

Let's delve into some practical advice and tips that can make all the difference when conducting love and relationship spells.

Tips for casting spells for love

- Set Clear Intentions : Spellcasting is all about setting clear and focused intentions. It's essential to know exactly what you desire before starting a love or relationship spell. Think deeply about what you want to manifest. Is it self-love, attracting a romantic partner, or improving an existing relationship? Be as specific as possible. Write down your intention if necessary. A well-defined intention is a powerful guiding force in spellcasting.

- Choose the Right Timing : Timing can be crucial when performing spells, especially those related to love and relationships. The waxing moon phase, which symbolizes growth and attraction, is often considered the best time to perform these spells. Also, consider performing your spell on a Friday, the day of the week associated with Venus, the goddess of love. Of course, the most powerful time is when you feel most connected to your intention.

- Select Appropriate Spell Components : The ingredients or components of your spell should align with your intention. For love spells, you might want to use rose quartz, known for its association with love, or herbs like rose or lavender, which have similar correspondences. Research your spell components carefully. The more the ingredients of your spell align with your intention, the more potent your spell will be.

- Believe in Your Spell : Faith is an essential aspect of successful spellcasting. When you cast your spell, believe in its power and its ability to manifest your desires. Doubt can hinder your results. After casting the spell, act as if your desired result is inevitable. This doesn't mean sitting back and waiting, but living your life as if the spell is already working.

- Consider the Ethics : Always consider the ethical implications of your spell. Remember the Wiccan Rede: "An it harm none, do what ye will." Avoid spells that manipulate another person's free will. Instead, focus on attracting the right love or improving yourself or your current relationship. Respect others' autonomy and feelings.

Remember, spell work isn't about taking shortcuts in life, but about aligning yourself with your goals and the natural energies of the universe. With clear intentions, right timing, appropriate components, unwavering belief, and ethical considerations, you can enhance the effectiveness of your love and relationship spells.

As we conclude this chapter on love and relationship spells, it's crucial to reflect on what we've learned and how it can be applied moving forward. This chapter was all about fostering self-love, strengthening relationships, and attracting love into our lives. Wiccan spells can be a powerful tool to guide these processes, offering a tangible way to manifest our intentions and desires.

However, let's remember that magic, including love spells, is not a shortcut or an easy way out of the complexities and difficulties that come with human relationships. The spells provided in this chapter are not meant to control others or impose our will on them. This goes against the Wiccan Rede of "Harm none, do what ye will". The essence of love and relationships lies in respect, consent, and mutual growth, values that should be upheld in our spellcasting.

When working with love spells, our focus should be on positive intentions: self-improvement, healing, understanding, patience, and love in its truest form. The spell for fostering self-love, for instance, is a tool for nurturing the most important relationship we have—the one with ourselves. By taking the time to nurture self-love, we allow ourselves to become better partners and build healthier relationships.

Likewise, the spell for strengthening relationships isn't about changing our partners or forcing a relationship to be something it's not. It's about focusing on our shared bonds, understanding, and love. The spell helps us channel our intentions to cultivate a more nurturing, patient, and loving relationship.

And finally, the spell for attracting love is not about luring a specific individual into our lives. Instead, it's about opening ourselves up to the universe and signaling that we're ready for love to find us. We're focusing our intentions on the kind of love we want to attract, thereby helping the universe align our path with that of another who shares these intentions.

If you're new to this, you might wonder if these spells truly work. Remember, magic in Wicca isn't like the immediate, dramatic magic often portrayed in movies or TV shows. Wiccan magic is subtle—it's about aligning our own energies with those of the natural world to bring about desired changes. It may take time, and the results may not always look exactly as we pictured. However, with patience, focus, and trust in the process, you'll find that these spells can be powerful aids in your journey of love and relationships.

Also, remember that spells are a part of the practice, not the whole. They work best when paired with actionable steps in our daily lives. If you cast a spell to strengthen your relationship, follow it up with real-world actions like open communication, spending quality time together, and showing empathy towards your partner. Similarly, if you're working with a spell to attract love, make sure you're also taking practical steps like socializing, meeting new people, and putting yourself out there.

Magic in Wicca is a beautiful, empowering practice. As you continue exploring this path, you'll likely find that casting these spells enhances not only your relationships with others but also your relationship with yourself. You're learning to focus your intentions, harness your inner power, and channel the energies around you. This is a transformative journey, one that takes time, practice, and plenty of patience.

Above all else, let the principles of love, respect, and harmony guide you in your practice. Whether you're working with spells or any other aspect of Wicca, these principles should be at the heart of what you do. As we move forward in this book, you'll learn more ways to incorporate these principles into your spellcasting and your daily life.

Keep practicing, stay open, and trust in the journey. Love in its many forms is a profound and transformative force, and through your practice, you're learning to invite more of it into your life. May your journey be filled with love, growth, and endless possibilities.

Spells for Prosperity and Success

A t times, we all find ourselves longing for a touch of prosperity or success, be it financial security, professional success, or achieving a long-held personal goal. Wicca, as a belief system, understands these desires, recognizing them as intrinsic parts of our human experience. As such, it's no surprise that there are spells specifically aimed to help manifest these desires into reality - the prosperity spells.

Prosperity spells are rituals designed to draw the energy of abundance and success into our lives. However, to properly utilize these spells, it's essential to first understand how they function within the Wiccan belief system.

In essence, every spell within Wicca revolves around the principle of intention. When you cast a spell, you're sending out a purposeful, concentrated intention into the universe. It's your desires, dreams, and aspirations that shape this intention. Consequently, in the case of prosperity spells, your intention is typically focused on attracting wealth, achieving success, or accomplishing certain goals.

It's crucial to note that the Wiccan interpretation of prosperity isn't limited to mere material wealth or success as defined by societal norms. Instead, prosperity in Wicca embraces a broader, more holistic meaning. It's about leading a fulfilling, balanced life where success is defined by personal satisfaction rather than external validation. It includes not just financial abundance but also emotional, mental, and spiritual wealth.

Further, casting spells in Wicca isn't about expecting instant, miraculous manifestations like in fairy tales. You can't cast a prosperity spell today and expect a sudden windfall tomorrow. Instead, these spells function by aligning our energies with universal energies of abundance and success. They pave the way for favorable circumstances and opportunities to manifest in our lives, thereby facilitating the realization of our desires.

When you cast a prosperity spell, you're essentially setting potent intentions and symbolically channeling these intentions into the universe. You're aligning yourself with your desired outcome, opening yourself up to opportunities that can help you achieve your goals, and invoking abundance and prosperity in your life.

The effectiveness of prosperity spells lies in their multi-level operation. Besides concentrating your intentions and energies, they act as a tangible reminder of your goals. Each time you perform a prosperity spell, it reinforces your ambitions, keeping them at the forefront of your consciousness. This constant reminder can significantly influence your everyday actions and decisions. In essence, the spell is both a spiritual practice and a practical tool for turning your desires into reality.

In the sections to follow, we'll delve into various prosperity spells designed to help you attract wealth, succeed in your work, and accomplish your personal goals. Remember, the effectiveness of these spells largely depends on your belief in them and your commitment to your intentions. Like any form of magic, it's essential to approach these spells with clarity of mind, openness of heart, and readiness of spirit.

As we delve deeper into the world of prosperity spells, it is essential to realize that these practices are not a one-size-fits-all magic trick for acquiring wealth and success. Instead, they are highly personal rituals that should align with your unique aspirations and the path you choose to follow. The essence of prosperity spells isn't about the mindless accumulation of wealth but about fostering a healthy relationship with abundance that aligns with your individual principles, ethics, and life goals.

With this understanding, let's explore some specific prosperity spells. Remember, these are examples, and you are encouraged to adjust them to fit your personal beliefs, preferences, and intentions. Magic, especially in Wicca, is a deeply personal journey, and it's entirely valid (and encouraged!) to tweak these practices to make them your own.

Before starting any spell, it's important to establish a clear intention. Take a moment to consider what prosperity and success truly mean to you. Perhaps it means financial security, achieving a certain career milestone, or succeeding in your personal projects. Your intention should resonate deeply with your aspirations, as it forms the core of your spell and directs the energy you'll be working with.

Let's look at a spell designed specifically to attract wealth. This spell leverages the power of symbolism, the moon phases, and your focused intent. Remember, this is just an example, so feel free to tweak it to suit your personal beliefs and needs.

The Abundance Drawing Moon Spell

You will need:

- 1 green candle

- Coins (preferably shiny and new)

- Cinnamon oil

- Small dish or saucer

- Paper and pen

Steps:

- Prepare your Space: Begin by cleansing your space. You might choose to do this with sage, sound, or simply by setting the intention of cleansing.

- Moon Phase: This spell is most effective when performed during the Waxing or Full Moon, when the moon's energy is potent for drawing in abundance.

- Setting up: On a small dish or saucer, place your green candle. Green is often associated with money and prosperity. Surround the base of the candle with coins. These act as a physical symbol of the wealth you're attracting.

- Anointing the Candle: Next, anoint your candle with cinnamon oil. As you do this, visualize wealth flowing towards you. Cinnamon is often associated with prosperity and success.

- Writing your Intention: On a piece of paper, write down the specific amount of wealth you wish to attract. Be as specific as you can. Fold the paper, turn 90 degrees, and fold it again. This is called a "quarter fold". Place it under the candle.

- Casting the Spell: Light the candle and focus on the flame. Visualize your life with the wealth you desire. Imagine it in as much detail as possible, feel the emotions you would feel, and believe in its manifestation. You can also say a chant or affirmation like, "Wealth and abundance flow to me, as I will, so mote it be."

- Closing the Spell: Allow the candle to burn down completely on its own to release your intention into the universe. Once the candle has burned out, take the folded paper and bury it in the earth, further symbolizing the growth of your wealth.

Remember to give gratitude to the universe and be patient. Spells work in harmony with the universe's timing, and results may not be instant. Also, continue to work towards your wealth goals in practical ways alongside your magical workings. Magic is a co-creative process that requires your active participation.

Let's explore a spell that's designed to boost success in your work or career. This is a spell you might use if you're looking for a promotion, new opportunities, or simply more satisfaction in your professional life. As always, feel free to modify the spell to fit your personal needs and beliefs.

The Career Advancement Charm Bag

You will need:

- 1 small bag or pouch (choose a color that signifies success to you, often gold or green)

- 1 piece of Aventurine or Citrine (both associated with success and prosperity)

- Bay leaves (known for their powerful magical properties in creating success and victory)

- Basil (attracts luck and success)

- Paper and pen

- Your favorite incense

Steps:

- Setting the Stage: Start by clearing your space physically and energetically. This can be done by tidying up, lighting incense, or using a cleansing herb like sage.

- Writing your Intent: On a small piece of paper, write your career-related wish. This could be as simple as "I am successful in my work" or specific like "I am promoted to the position of Senior Manager".

- Creating the Charm Bag: Take your bag or pouch and hold it in your hands. Visualize it filling with radiant, golden light – this is the energy of success.

- Adding the Ingredients: Place the Aventurine or Citrine stone in the bag, envisioning it as a magnet for career success. Next, add in the bay leaves and basil. As you do so, visualize these herbs amplifying your intentions, bringing victory, luck, and success in your work. Lastly, fold your written intent and place it in the bag. As you place each item, feel the energy of success growing stronger.

- Sealing the Bag: Draw the bag closed and hold it in your hands. Say a simple affirmation or chant such as, "I succeed in my work, my career advances with ease, as I will it, so mote it be."

- Using the Charm Bag: Keep this bag in your workspace, in your purse, or in a pocket – anywhere you'll be reminded of your intent regularly. Feel its energy surrounding you whenever you work.

- Refreshing the Bag: Every new moon, consider refreshing the charm bag. You can do this by removing the items, cleansing them (placing them in moonlight is an easy way), and then placing them back in the bag with your renewed intent for success.

Remember, spell work is all about setting intentions and sending them into the universe, but you also have to take action! So, alongside this spell, make sure you are also taking practical steps towards your career advancement.

Of course, let's explore a simple but powerful spell to help you focus your intentions and energy on achieving your goals. This spell can be modified to suit any goal you have, be it related to personal development, relationships, finances, or health.

The Goal Manifestation Candle Spell

You will need:

- 1 white or gold candle (white for all-purpose, gold for achievement and success)

- A piece of paper and a pen

- Essential oil (such as frankincense for success, rosemary for clarity, or any scent that aligns with your goal)

- Herbs or crystals associated with your goal (optional)

- A fire-safe container or dish

Steps:

- Clearing your Space: Begin by creating a peaceful and clear space where you can focus on your spell work. Clean up if necessary, turn off any distracting electronics, and maybe put on some soft background music if it helps you concentrate.

- Preparing your Candle: Take your candle and rub a small amount of essential oil onto it, visualizing your goal as you do so. This act charges the candle with your intention.

- Writing your Goal: On your piece of paper, write down your goal in as specific and positive terms as you can. Instead of writing "I want to be debt-free," write "I am financially independent and secure." The language we use can greatly impact the effectiveness of our spell.

- Charging your Spell: Hold the candle in your hands and focus on your goal. Visualize yourself achieving this goal. See the success, feel the joy and satisfaction. Pour all these feelings into the candle.

- Casting your Spell: Place the candle in a safe place and light it. As you do so, say out loud or in your head: "As I light this candle, my goal is brought into light. As it burns, so does my will to achieve. As I speak, so I create." Allow the candle to burn down completely in a safe place. Some people prefer to do this all in one night, others prefer to light the candle for a few minutes each day as they focus on their goal.

- Disposing of the Remnants: After the candle has burned down, dispose of the remnants respectfully. Bury them in the earth, throw them in running water, or simply place them in the trash, whatever feels right to you.

Remember, the true magic of this spell comes from the clarity of your goal and the power of your intention. While the candle and other tools can enhance your spell, they are not the source of the magic – you are. As you go through your day, remember your goal and take actions that bring you closer to achieving it. The universe works in mysterious ways, and often, the path to our goal becomes clearer once we've made that firm commitment to achieving it.

Tips for Prosperity Spells

Now, let's delve into some essential advice and practical tips for success when performing prosperity and success spells.

- **Clarity in Goals** : Just as in love spells, it's crucial to be clear and specific about what kind of prosperity or success you want to attract. Are you looking for financial prosperity? Career success? Academic achievement? The more specific you are, the better you can tailor your spell and the more likely it will manifest your desired outcome. Write down your goals and visualize them as part of your spellcasting process to enhance your focus.

- **Choose Appropriate Spell Components** : When it comes to prosperity and success spells, certain components are particularly potent. Consider using green candles, a color associated with growth and abundance, or crystals such as citrine and green aventurine, known for their wealth-attracting

properties. Herbs like cinnamon and clover are also traditionally used in prosperity spells. Aligning the components
of your spell with your intention will enhance its power.

- **Alignment with Real-World Efforts** : Your spell work
  should go hand in hand with your efforts in the physical
  world. For example, if you're performing a spell for career
  success, you should also be updating your resume or seeking
  new opportunities. Spells can create opportunities and align
  energies in your favor, but it's still up to you to take the
  necessary actions to manifest your desires.

- **Maintain a Positive Attitude** : Maintain a positive attitude
  and a mindset of abundance when performing prosperity
  and success spells. If you're focusing on lack or approaching
  your spell work with a mindset of desperation, you may
  hinder your results. Try to cultivate a feeling of gratitude for
  the abundance already present in your life, however small it
  may seem.

- **Patience and Perseverance** : Results from prosperity and
  success spells may not be instant. Sometimes, it takes time for
  the energies to align and for opportunities to present themselves. Be patient and don't get discouraged if you don't see
  immediate results. Keep your focus on your intention, continue to put in the necessary effort, and trust in the process.

By focusing on your goals, using appropriate spell components,
aligning your spell work with your real-world efforts, maintaining a
positive attitude, and practicing patience, you'll be well on your way
to successfully casting prosperity and success spells.

In our journey into the mystical world of prosperity and success spells, we've encountered the fascinating process of crafting and casting spells that manifest our deepest desires. As we reflect on this journey, it's important to remember that spellcasting is, at its core, a tool for focusing intention and harnessing the universe's natural energies to foster our aspirations.

One of the key ideas we've explored is the notion that prosperity and success aren't purely financial or career-based concepts. They encompass every aspect of our lives, from our personal development and relationships to our wellbeing and spiritual growth. Spells, in this context, are a versatile method for working toward a variety of goals, providing a tangible means of putting our intentions out into the universe.

We delved into the mechanics of prosperity spells, understanding their ability to align our intentions with the universe's abundance. Using specific tools, symbols, and ritual actions, these spells allow us to become more attuned to the energies of prosperity and success, fostering our growth and development in these areas.

We then explored three unique spells, each one designed to attract wealth, success in work, and goal achievement. Through these examples, we saw how each spell is personalized to the caster's unique goals and desires, reinforcing the idea that our own personal energy and intentions are integral to the spellcasting process.

As we conclude this chapter, it's crucial to note that the true effectiveness of these spells lies not in the words we utter or the items we use but in the clarity of our intentions and our belief in the possibility of our desired outcomes. The universe is a vast web of interconnected energies, and our thoughts and desires are a part of this vibrant network. When we cast a spell, we are tapping into this network, directing the energies towards our intentions.

As you continue your journey in Wicca, remember that spellcasting is a personal and intimate process. There's no right or wrong way to cast a spell, and the most powerful spells are often those that come from the heart. Feel free to adapt the spells presented in this chapter to better suit your personal circumstances or preferences.

Moreover, keep in mind that patience and perseverance are key. Sometimes, the universe takes time to align with our desires, and success may not come instantly. Trust in the process and maintain a positive mindset, for as the saying goes, "As you sow, so shall you reap."

In the next chapter, we'll explore a new dimension of spellcasting: spells for healing and well-being. These spells will provide another set of tools for you to enhance your life, promoting physical health, emotional stability, and overall happiness. As we continue our exploration of Wicca, we'll discover even more about the profound power that lies within us and the natural world around us.

In the end, remember that every step you take on this path brings you closer to understanding your place in the universe, helping you to live in harmony with nature and your true self. So, keep your intentions clear, your heart open, and your mind focused as we delve further into the beautiful realm of Wicca.

Spells for Healing and Well-being

Welcome to the eighth chapter of our journey into the world of Wicca and its spellcasting practices. Having explored the realms of love, prosperity, and success, we now turn our attention to an equally vital aspect of life: health and well-being. This chapter will provide a deep dive into the world of healing spells, focusing on how they can aid both emotional and physical health.

In many ways, our well-being forms the very core of our existence. It determines how we feel, how we function, and how we interact with the world around us. When we're in good health, we're able to live our lives to the fullest, pursuing our dreams and enjoying our relationships. However, when our health is compromised, either physically or emotionally, it can cast a shadow over our entire existence.

That's where the power of healing spells comes in. Wicca, with its deep connection to the natural world and its energies, offers us an array of spellcasting practices to promote health and well-being. It provides us with ways to tap into the natural energies around us, guiding them to heal, restore, and revitalize ourselves.

Before we delve into the specifics of these healing spells, it's crucial to understand the Wiccan perspective on health and healing. Unlike some modern approaches to health that compartmentalize the body and mind, Wicca sees health as a holistic concept. The physical, emotional, mental, and spiritual aspects of our being are all interconnected, each one influencing and being influenced by the others. Therefore, healing spells in Wicca often target not just physical ailments but also emotional distress, mental instability, and spiritual disconnection.

In the world of Wicca, healing spells are seen as a way of restoring balance and harmony. Illness, stress, and emotional turmoil are viewed as imbalances in our natural state, disruptions in the natural flow of energy within and around us. Healing spells aim to correct these imbalances, drawing on the natural energies of the universe to restore us to a state of health and wholeness.

An important note is that Wiccan healing spells are not meant to replace conventional medical treatment. They should be seen as complementary to any treatments prescribed by healthcare professionals. They provide a spiritual and emotional aspect to healing that can enhance physical treatments, but they should not be used in lieu of professional medical advice.

As we embark on this exploration of healing spells, we'll learn about various types of spells designed to promote physical healing, alleviate emotional distress, and restore balance to our lives. We'll discover the power of herbs, crystals, candles, and other tools in facilitating these healing processes, and we'll learn how to harness these energies to enhance our own health and well-being.

Whether you're seeking to heal from a physical illness, cope with emotional pain, or simply want to maintain good health and a balanced state of being, healing spells offer a powerful tool. By learning to tap into the natural energies of the universe, you can take an active role in your own healing process, fostering a state of health and well-being that aligns with the natural world.

In the practice of Wicca, healing spells are more than just rituals. They represent the harmony between the practitioner and the universe and the belief in the power of nature to heal and restore. Healing, in the context of Wicca, goes beyond just physical ailments and extends into the realm of emotional, mental, and spiritual well-being. It's about aligning yourself with the natural rhythms and energies of the universe to create a state of balance and harmony within.

This understanding of health and healing is deeply rooted in the principles of Wicca itself. As we've already explored in previous chapters, Wicca is a religion that reveres nature and respects the interconnectedness of all things. This principle is reflected in its approach to healing, which sees the individual as an integral part of the universe, with health being a state of balance with the natural energies that surround and permeate us.

It's worth noting that the Wiccan concept of healing resonates with many modern understandings of health and well-being, especially in the field of holistic and integrative medicine. The mind-body connection, the importance of emotional health in physical well-being, the impact of our environment on our health - these are all ideas that are being increasingly recognized and validated by modern science.

Now, let's delve into the realm of healing spells themselves. These spells can range from simple rituals to intricate ceremonies, depending on the tradition and the individual practitioner. They often involve the use of various tools and ingredients, such as candles, herbs, crystals, and incantations, which serve to focus the practitioner's intention and channel the energy towards healing.

In the following sections, we will explore some specific examples of healing spells. These spells will cover various aspects of health and well-being, from promoting physical healing to reducing stress and enhancing overall wellness. These examples are designed to provide you with a practical understanding of how healing spells work and how you can incorporate them into your own Wiccan practice.

While the spells described in this chapter can be powerful tools for healing, it's important to remember that the true power of any spell lies in the intention and focus of the practitioner. As we've discussed in previous chapters, the act of casting a spell is really about aligning your intention with the natural energies of the universe. When it comes to healing spells, this means focusing your intention on health, balance, and well-being and trusting in the power of nature to bring about the desired outcome.

Lastly, as we delve into these spells, I encourage you to approach them with an open mind and a respectful heart. Wiccan healing spells are deeply spiritual practices that are rooted in a reverence for nature and a belief in the interconnectedness of all things. By approaching them with a sense of respect and reverence, you can align yourself more fully with their energies and enhance their effectiveness.

Spell for Promoting Healing

You will need:

- 1 Blue candle

- Healing oil (e.g., lavender oil or eucalyptus oil)

- Piece of clear quartz crystal

Instructions:

- Cleanse and Prepare your Space: Before you begin your spell, ensure that your area is clean and free from any negative energies. You might want to smudge your space using sage or palo santo, or simply clean the room and visualize any negativity being swept away.

- Ground and Center Yourself: Sit comfortably in your space. Close your eyes, breathe deeply, and visualize your connection to the earth and the sky. Imagine roots growing down from your feet into the earth and branches reaching up to the sky from your head. Feel the energy flowing through you and know that you are connected to the universe.

- Set Your Intention: Light the blue candle, representing healing and tranquility. As you do so, state your intention for this spell. You might say something like: "I light this candle to tap into the healing energies of the universe. May the flame guide my path to health and wellness."

- Charge the Crystal: Hold the clear quartz in your hands and visualize it glowing with a healing light. Speak your intention into the crystal, imagining that your words are imbuing it with power. You might say: "I charge this crystal with the healing energies of the universe. May it amplify my intention and guide my path to health."

- Anoint the Candle: Dip your finger in the healing oil and anoint the candle with it, drawing from the base to the wick. This action symbolizes drawing in healing energy.

- Meditate and Visualize Healing: Once your candle is lit and your crystal charged, take a few moments to meditate on your intention. Close your eyes and visualize the healing energy entering your body, flowing through every cell, and promoting healing and wellness. Feel the energy from the candle and crystal amplifying your intention.

- Close the Spell: When you feel ready, thank the universe for its healing energies and blow out your candle. Know that your intention has been heard and is being acted upon. Leave the crystal in a place where you will see it regularly to remind you of your healing intentions.

Remember, this spell isn't meant to replace any current medical treatments or professional advice. It's a spiritual tool meant to supplement and support whatever healing journey you are on. It's a way to focus your personal energy on recovery and healing, tapping into the healing properties that are so inherent in nature and the Wiccan tradition.

Spell for Reducing Stress

You will need:

- 1 Lavender candle

- Essential oil diffuser (optional)

- Lavender oil (optional)

- Amethyst crystal

Instructions:

- Prepare Your Space: As with any ritual, begin by cleansing your space. You can do this physically by tidying up the area or energetically using sage, incense, or any method you prefer. Create a calm, safe space where you can focus your energy.

- Ground Yourself: Sit comfortably and close your eyes. Take a few deep breaths, focusing on the sensation of your breath entering and leaving your body. Envision yourself as a tree with roots extending deep into the earth, anchoring you and providing stability.

- Light the Candle: Light your lavender candle. As you do so, articulate your intention, saying something like, "With the lighting of this candle, I invite calm and peace into my life."

- Diffuse Lavender Oil: If you have a diffuser and lavender oil, this is a good time to set it running. Lavender is known for its stress-relieving properties and using it in this way can enhance the effect of the spell.

- Hold the Amethyst: Take the amethyst crystal in your hand. Amethyst is a crystal associated with peace, healing, and stress relief. Feel its coolness and envision the stone absorbing the stress and tension from your body.

- Meditate: As you hold the amethyst, visualize your stress as a dark cloud within you. With each exhale, envision this cloud leaving your body and being absorbed by the amethyst. With each inhale, envision calming, peaceful energy entering your body. Repeat this until you feel a noticeable difference in your stress levels.

- Close the Spell: When you feel ready, extinguish the candle and thank the universe for the peace it has brought you. Keep the amethyst nearby as a tangible reminder of your intention to maintain a sense of calm.

Please remember, this spell is a form of stress relief and not a substitute for professional help. If you're feeling persistently stressed or anxious, please seek guidance from a healthcare professional.

Tips for healing spells

Here are some practical tips for success when performing health and wellness spells.

- **Clear Intention** : As with any spell work, clarity in your intention is paramount. Define the type of healing you're seeking, whether it's physical, emotional, or spiritual. Are you looking for general wellbeing or aiming to alleviate a specific ailment? Visualize the outcome you desire and incorporate this into your spell.

- **Choose Your Components Mindfully** : Use elements known for their healing properties. Crystals like clear quartz or amethyst, herbs such as rosemary and lavender, and colors like blue and green can all contribute to health and wellness spells. Use these elements in ways that feel right to you.

- **Align Your Spell work with Real-World Actions** : Magic should not replace professional medical advice and treatment. It's crucial to align your spell work with any treatment plans or lifestyle changes recommended by healthcare professionals. Consider your spells as a way to enhance or support these efforts, not replace them.

- **Cultivate a Healing Mindset** : As you perform your spell, foster a positive attitude and visualize your body (or mind) healing. Mindset can play a significant role in health and wellness. By aligning your thoughts with your intentions, you can create a powerful catalyst for healing.

- **Patience and Compassion**: Healing often takes time, and it's crucial to be patient with the process. Practice self-compassion, allowing yourself to rest and recover without rushing or judging the process. Your spellwork can help maintain this nurturing, supportive mindset throughout your healing journey.

By focusing on your intention, choosing appropriate components, aligning your spell work with real-world actions, fostering a healing mindset, and being patient with the process, you'll increase the efficacy of your health and wellness spells. Remember, your journey towards better health is a process, and your magic is a powerful tool to guide and support you along the way.

Conclusion

As we reach the end of this enlightening chapter, it's crucial to understand the profound power and potential healing spells can hold. When cast mindfully and with a genuine intention, they can significantly contribute to our overall emotional and physical health. Whether it's a spell to promote healing, reduce stress, or foster overall well-being, each serves as a tool to help us navigate through the journey of life more effectively.

What makes these healing spells particularly potent is the energy that we pour into them. This energy, rooted in our sincere desires for healing and transformation, serves as the driving force that directs the natural forces around us towards our stated objectives. It's this energy that resonates with the universe's harmonious energy and helps bring about the desired changes.

Remember, the focus on well-being is an integral part of Wiccan practice. It aligns with the religion's reverence for life and nature, acknowledging that our well-being is interconnected with the world around us. The spells we've explored are, therefore, much more than symbolic actions; they are an embodiment of this deep-seated respect for life and our desire to live harmoniously with the cycles of nature.

Moreover, as you've learned to cast these spells, you've also, in essence, learned to take charge of your life. You've learned to harness the power within and around you to transform your reality. And that is a skill that can prove beneficial in many areas of life. Whether you're facing health issues, struggling with stress, or simply striving for overall wellness, these spells can provide a supportive hand.

However, it's important to remember that while these spells can aid us, they're not a substitute for medical attention or professional help. They should be seen as a complementary tool rather than a primary solution, especially for serious or persistent health problems. If you or someone you know is facing such challenges, it's vital to reach out to healthcare professionals.

In addition, while casting these spells, always remember the Wiccan Rede: "An' it harm none, do what ye will." Ensure that your intentions are pure, your actions harm no one, and that you're not infringing upon another's free will. We must respect individual autonomy and understand that our spells should not manipulate others' feelings, thoughts, or actions.

As you continue to learn and grow in your Wiccan practice, I encourage you to incorporate these healing spells into your routine. Experiment with them, adapt them to fit your needs, and see how they work for you. Note your feelings, your successes, and even the spells that don't seem to work. Each of these experiences will provide valuable insights and contribute to your growth as a Wiccan practitioner.

And finally, remember to have patience. Just like healing in the physical world, spiritual and emotional healing also takes time. It's a process that unfolds gradually. So, give yourself the time and space to heal, to grow, and to embrace the wonderful journey that lies ahead.

In the next chapter, we will explore protection spells and how they can shield us from negative energies. These spells are essential tools for safeguarding ourselves and maintaining our well-being, making them a vital addition to your Wiccan practice. As always, approach them with an open mind, respect for the Wiccan principles, and a sincere intention to learn and grow. I look forward to guiding you through this exciting next phase of your Wiccan journey.

Protection Spells and Warding off Negative Energies

In our exploration of Wiccan practices and beliefs thus far, we've delved into the power of spells that can influence various aspects of our lives - love, prosperity, healing, and well-being. In this chapter, we turn our attention to a crucial and highly impactful type of magic that lies at the core of Wiccan practices – protection spells. These spells serve as essential tools that safeguard us from negative energies and create a spiritual shield that reinforces our personal safety and peace.

Protection spells have been a vital part of spiritual and magical traditions across various cultures and epochs. These protective measures are more than simple charms; they symbolize our inner strength and resilience, our ability to stand up against forces that may seek to harm us, and our power to create a harmonious space for ourselves and our loved ones. Protection spells, like all spells, operate on the principles of intention and energy. When we focus our intention on creating a safe and protected space, and when we direct our energy towards this goal, we can effectively ward off negativity and harm.

There are various types of protection spells, each with its unique attributes and uses. Some spells focus on warding off specific negative energies or entities, while others create a general protective shield around the practitioner or their space. These spells can be used to safeguard our homes, protect us during our magical practices, or shield us from negativity in our day-to-day lives.

The importance of protection spells in Wiccan practice cannot be overstated. Wicca is a religion that teaches its followers to be in harmony with nature and the universe. However, just as nature consists of both nurturing and destructive forces, the universe, too, is a mix of positive and negative energies. While we strive to align ourselves with positive energies to manifest love, prosperity, healing, and well-being, we must also protect ourselves from the negative energies that exist.

Just as a doctor would not perform a surgery without first ensuring the sterility of their environment, a Wiccan practitioner should not perform spells without first securing their spiritual environment. Protection spells serve as this necessary measure of safety, ensuring that we ward off any negative or harmful influences that could potentially disrupt our practices or our lives.

However, it's vital to understand that protection spells are not about fostering fear or paranoia. They are not meant to make us constantly wary of negative forces lurking around every corner. Instead, they encourage a sense of empowerment and security. They affirm our ability to defend ourselves spiritually and ensure that our practices and our lives are free from unnecessary disruptions or influences.

Furthermore, protection spells also align with the core Wiccan belief in personal responsibility. As Wiccans, we believe in our ability to influence our circumstances and our lives. We acknowledge that we have the power to attract positive influences and repel negative ones. By casting protection spells, we take proactive steps to guard our energy and our space, embodying the self-determining spirit at the heart of Wiccan practice.

In this chapter, we will explore various types of protection spells. We will delve into spells for warding off negativity, spells for protection from harm, and spells for creating a protective shield. Each of these spells will serve as a valuable tool in your Wiccan toolkit, helping you to create a secure and harmonious environment for your practice and your life. Let's begin this journey of learning and empowerment together.

Now that we have laid out a thorough understanding of what protection spells are, let's delve into the mechanics of how they work. We cannot emphasize enough that Wiccan magic, including protection spells, is not about summoning external powers to do our bidding. Rather, it's about working in harmony with natural forces and our own inherent potential to create change. In other words, protection spells are not about warding off an external enemy, but about fortifying our internal defenses and resilience.

We are all made of energy, and we all interact with the energies around us, whether we consciously realize it or not. Protection spells work by helping us to consciously align ourselves with positive energies and disconnect from negative ones. When we cast a protection spell, we are setting an intention and channeling our energy to create a protective shield around us or a specific area. This shield serves to repel negative or harmful energies while attracting positive ones.

However, it's crucial to keep in mind that protection spells, like all Wiccan practices, require respect for free will and should not be used to manipulate or control others. Remember the Wiccan Rede – "An it harm none, do what ye will." A protection spell should never cause harm or infringe upon another's free will. It should not be used to cause harm to someone who you perceive as a threat, but rather to reinforce your own spiritual defenses and resilience.

Protection spells come in various forms and can be tailored to suit different needs and situations. For instance, there are protection spells to safeguard your home, creating a peaceful and safe space for you and your loved ones. There are spells to protect you during travel, warding off potential risks and ensuring your journey is smooth and safe. There are even spells to protect your dreams, warding off nightmares and ensuring restful sleep.

These spells often incorporate various tools and elements to aid in the spellcasting process. For example, candles, crystals, and herbs might be used, each chosen for their specific protective properties. The color of a candle, the type of crystal, and the choice of herb all play a role in the efficacy of a protection spell.

In the following sections, we will provide examples of some of these protective spells. We will explain how to prepare for the spell, the items you will need, the best time to perform the spell, and the steps to follow. As we explore these spells, always remember the importance of intention. Your intention is your most potent tool in spellcasting. It is your focused will and desire for protection that gives power to your spell.

Whether you are new to Wiccan practices or an experienced practitioner, understanding and utilizing protection spells can enhance your spiritual practice and your personal sense of security. These spells offer more than just spiritual protection; they provide a way for you to take control of your energy and your environment, fostering a deep sense of empowerment and peace.

In the next sections, we will delve into examples of protection spells, each tailored to ward off different types of negativity, provide protection from harm, and create a protective shield. Let's delve into these powerful practices together and fortify our spiritual defenses.

Spell for Warding Off Negativity

You will need:

- A black candle (black is associated with banishing and absorbing negativity)

- Salt (a well-known purifier)

- Smudge stick or incense (sage or lavender work well for cleansing)

- A small piece of paper and a pen

- A fireproof bowl or dish

Instructions:

- Begin by creating a calm and peaceful environment for your spell work. This can be your personal altar, a quiet corner of your home, or any space where you feel safe and comfortable.

- Light the smudge stick or incense. As the smoke begins to waft around you, visualize it carrying away any negative energies clinging to you or your space. You may want to say a simple chant or affirmation as you do this, such as, "Only peace remains here. Negativity has no place."

- Take the black candle in your hands and focus your intention on it. Envision the flame of the candle as a beacon, absorbing and banishing all negative energy. Light the candle.

- On the small piece of paper, write down what you wish to banish from your life – this could be a specific worry, fear, situation, or even a general sense of negativity.

- Carefully, and with your intention firmly in mind, burn the piece of paper in the flame of the black candle. As you do this, visualize your negative energy transferring to the paper, and being consumed by the flame.

- Once the paper has burned, collect the ashes and mix them with a pinch of salt in the fireproof dish. As you mix, imagine the salt neutralizing and purifying the negativity that the ashes represent.

- Finally, dispose of the ashes and salt, ideally by returning them to the earth. As you do this, envision the negativity being absorbed and neutralized by the earth. You could say something like, "I release this negativity, and return it to the earth for transformation and renewal."

- Close your spell by thanking any energies or deities you called upon, and by grounding yourself – this could be as simple as taking a few deep breaths, having a meal, or taking a short walk.

Remember that the power of this spell lies in your intention. It's important to focus your will on banishing negativity throughout the process. Always remember the law of threefold return and ensure your actions and intentions are aimed at causing no harm.

Spell for Protection from Harm

You will need:

- A white candle (white represents purity and protection)

- A piece of paper and a pen

- Sea salt (a purifying element)

- A protective stone, such as black tourmaline or obsidian

- A small cloth bag or pouch

Instructions:

- Choose a calm and peaceful environment where you will not be disturbed. This can be your personal altar, a quiet room, or any space where you feel secure and comfortable.

- Begin by centering and grounding yourself. You can do this by taking a few deep breaths, imagining roots growing from your feet into the earth, or visualizing a protective light surrounding you.

- Light the white candle and say, "With this light, I invoke protection. May its glow keep me safe from harm."

- On the piece of paper, write a phrase that encapsulates your desire for protection. It could be something like, "I am safe from all harm," or, "I am protected on all sides."

- Place the piece of paper on a flat surface and sprinkle a circle of sea salt around it. As you do so, visualize the salt creating a barrier of protection around your written intention.

- Hold the protective stone in your hand. Close your eyes and envision a protective energy emanating from the stone. Say, "I charge this stone with protective energy, to keep me safe from harm."

- Place the stone on top of the paper within the salt circle.

Leave the stone there and allow the candle to burn out on its own (make sure this is done in a safe manner).

- Once the candle has burned out, fold the paper around the stone and place them in the small cloth bag or pouch. Keep this with you or in a safe place to serve as a protective talisman.

Remember, the power of your spell comes from your intention and belief. Approach your spell work with a clear mind and sincere heart. As always, bear in mind the Wiccan Rede and the rule of threefold return – your magic should harm none and be for the highest good of all involved.

Spell for Creating a Protective Shield

You will need:

- A piece of clear quartz (for clarity and amplification of intention)

- A piece of black obsidian or black tourmaline (for protection)

- A white candle (for purity and protection)

- A sage bundle or incense (for purification and protection)

- A small bowl of water (representing the element of Water)

- A small dish of salt (representing the element of Earth)

Instructions:

- Find a quiet and comfortable space where you will not be disturbed. Take a moment to center and ground yourself.

- Light the white candle and the sage or incense. As the smoke begins to waft, imagine it carrying away any negative energy from you and your space.

- Hold the piece of clear quartz in your dominant hand and say, "I imbue this quartz with my intention: to create a protective shield around me, safeguarding me from any harm."

- Take the piece of black obsidian or tourmaline in your other hand and say, "I charge this stone with the power to repel all negative energies, to serve as my protective shield."

- Next, take the bowl of water in your hands. Visualize the water washing over you, cleansing you of any remaining negative energy and bringing you peace. Say, "With this element of water, I cleanse and protect."

- Then, take the dish of salt in your hands. Visualize the salt grounding you and solidifying your protective shield. Say, "With this element of earth, I ground and protect."

- Arrange the quartz, obsidian (or tourmaline), bowl of water, and dish of salt in a circle around the white candle. As you place each item, visualize a protective sphere forming around you, strong and impenetrable.

- Once your circle is complete, sit quietly and visualize this protective shield around you, glowing with a warm light, strong and solid, impervious to any harm.

- To end the ritual, thank the elements and your protective stones for their aid. Blow out the candle, and keep the stones somewhere safe where they will not be disturbed.

Remember, the effectiveness of this spell lies in your belief and your intention. Always use magic responsibly, and in accordance with the Wiccan Rede. Harm none, and remember the Threefold Law. As you grow in your practice, you'll find that your protective shield grows stronger too.

Tips for protection spells

Here are some pointers to ensure success in casting spells for protection and warding.

- **Clarify Your Need for Protection** : The first step in successful protection and warding spells is understanding what you need protection from. It could be negative energy, harmful intentions, or even your own fears and insecurities. Being clear about what you want to ward off will allow you to create a more focused and effective spell.

- **Select Suitable Materials** : For protection spells, consider incorporating elements traditionally associated with protection. These can include crystals like black tourmaline and obsidian, herbs such as basil and rosemary, and symbols like the pentagram or the eye of Horus. Research these elements and choose those that resonate with you.

- **Balance Protection with Invitation** : Remember, protection isn't just about keeping things out. It's also about creating a safe space for positivity and growth. As you cast your spell, consider what you want to invite into your life as you ward off negativity.

- **Maintain Your Protective Measures** : Protection spells aren't always a one-and-done deal. Some may need to be renewed periodically, especially if you've been exposed to a lot of negativity or have been through a particularly challenging period. Regularly cleansing your space and aura can also help maintain your protective barriers.

- **Trust in Your Power** : Believe in your ability to protect yourself. Trust that your spell work will be effective and that you have the power to create a safe, positive environment for yourself. Remember, the power of magic lies within you.

By clarifying your needs, choosing suitable materials, balancing protection with invitation, maintaining your protective measures, and trusting in your power, you'll be well on your way to crafting effective protection and warding spells. Your safety and wellbeing are paramount, and these tips will aid you in crafting the protective magic you need.

As we conclude this chapter on protection spells and warding off negative energies, it is crucial to underscore that the heart of Wiccan practice is not only about casting spells but equally about fostering a deep spiritual connection with the world around us. This understanding is intrinsic to the art of creating protective boundaries through spells and rituals, which are much more than mere mechanical actions. They are intimate expressions of our relationships with the universe and our roles within it.

The act of casting protection spells and creating wards against negative energies is both a spiritual and a psychological process. From a spiritual perspective, we invite protective energies and use our intention to manifest a shield that can safeguard us from harm. From a psychological perspective, these actions reinforce our mind's conviction that we are in control of our surroundings, helping us foster resilience against adversities.

The spells described in this chapter are illustrative examples, and like many other aspects of Wicca, they are not set in stone. Their power lies in the intention behind them and in the personal significance they hold for the practitioner. As you move forward on your Wiccan path, feel free to adapt these spells or create your own, guided by your intuition and your unique connection to the elements and energies around you.

In our journey through Wicca, it is essential to remember that while spells can be powerful tools for creating change, they should not be used as a substitute for practical action. If we find ourselves facing repeated negativity, it may be a sign that we need to make changes on a more mundane level, such as reconsidering the environments we place ourselves in or the relationships we maintain. Similarly, a protection spell should not replace taking practical measures to ensure our physical safety.

This chapter's focus has been on spells that ward off negativity and protect against harm, and they serve as a reminder that we are not passive observers in our lives. Instead, we are active participants with the power to shape our experiences and the energy that surrounds us. While the world may be full of forces beyond our control, through intention and will, we can significantly influence our immediate surroundings and our perception of the world.

As we close, consider this: every spell you cast is a testament to your strength and an affirmation of your personal power. It is a declaration to the universe that you are a being of intention and resolve, capable of channeling divine energies to effect change in your life. Remember this as you move forward on your path. The act of casting a spell is a sacred one, imbued with the power of your spirit, the energies around you, and the rich lineage of Wiccan wisdom that informs your practice.

In the end, the journey into Wicca is an exploration of self, and your spell work is a reflection of that. Remember to respect your intuition and use your power wisely and ethically, always with an awareness of the Wiccan Rede and the Threefold Law. With this in mind, may your path be filled with growth, discovery, and a profound connection to the magic that surrounds you.

As we move on to the next chapters, keep the lessons of this one close to heart, for protection and warding off negative energies will continue to be an integral part of your Wiccan practice. Carry forward this knowledge, always striving to live in harmony with the world around you, treading gently upon the Earth, and remaining ever conscious of the energy you contribute to the universe.

Troubleshooting
Your Spells

As we begin Chapter 10, it's important to address some of the challenges that may arise as you embark upon your journey into the world of spellcasting. Even for the most seasoned practitioners, spells sometimes don't manifest as expected. Like any craft, spellcasting is a practice where learning is ongoing and mistakes are inevitable. It is through these trials that we deepen our understanding, learn to refine our techniques, and grow in our connection with the energies we seek to channel.

The first common issue that beginners might face when casting spells is the sense of doubt. Doubt about one's abilities, doubt about the effectiveness of the spell, or even doubt about the legitimacy of spellcasting itself. Wicca and spellcasting are deeply spiritual practices that require faith, not in the religious sense, but in the sense of trust in oneself and the energies one seeks to harness. In essence, spellcasting is a conversation with the universe. If you enter this conversation filled with doubt, it's akin to mumbling your words or not speaking clearly. The universe responds to clear intentions and confidence.

If you find doubt creeping in, take a moment to ground yourself. Remember your connection to the divine energies around you. Recall the feeling of the Earth beneath your feet, the warmth of the Sun on your skin, the breath of the Wind against your cheek, and the flow of Water in a nearby stream. You are a part of this universe, and you have the right to engage with it. Meditate on this and let your doubt dissolve into this broader sense of connection.

The second issue is that of rushed or haphazard preparation. Spell-casting is not merely about reciting words and burning candles. It's about creating a sacred space, setting a clear intention, and bringing together symbolic elements in a way that speaks to the subconscious mind and to the energies you're working with. Skimping on this process or rushing through it can result in a spell that lacks focus or potency.

Therefore, before beginning any spell, take the time to fully understand the spell you're casting. Research the meanings of the tools and ingredients you're using. Know why each element is there and what it represents. Make sure your sacred space is clean, calm, and free of distractions. Meditate on your intention, visualizing it clearly in your mind. It's not about the time it takes but the care and reverence with which you approach the spellcasting process.

A third challenge that can arise when casting spells is a lack of patience. Especially in our modern world where instant gratification is often expected, it can be easy to feel disappointed if a spell doesn't yield immediate results. But the universe works in its own time. A seed does not become a flower overnight; it requires time to absorb nutrients, to grow, and to eventually blossom. Similarly, the energy set forth by your spell needs time to align circumstances, opportunities, and events to manifest your intention.

Moreover, the effectiveness of a spell also depends on your actions in the physical world. For instance, a spell to find a new job will be less effective if you're not also actively seeking employment, updating your resume, or pursuing opportunities. Spells are not standalone solutions; they work best when coupled with practical efforts in the material realm.

Finally, it's possible that a spell might not work because it's not the right spell for your intention, or it might be conflicting with a higher purpose or lesson you need to learn. In this case, it's essential to remember that the universe operates with a vast perspective that sees beyond our individual desires. The purpose of spellcasting is not to impose our will on the world, but to align ourselves with the flow of the universe and to tap into the currents of power and potential that exist around us.

As you delve deeper into the art of spellcasting, remember that challenges are not roadblocks, but stepping stones leading you toward a deeper understanding of your craft. They invite you to explore, to question, and to refine your practice. Keep an open mind and a patient heart, for spellcasting is a dance with the universe, a dialogue with energies seen and unseen, and above all, a journey of discovery.

What to do when a spell doesn't work.

With the understanding that the art of spellcasting is a journey full of learning opportunities, let's further delve into the troubleshooting methods that can assist you when a spell doesn't produce the desired outcome.

One vital aspect to consider when a spell doesn't seem to be working is the clarity and specificity of your intention. A well-crafted spell is driven by a clear, focused intention. It's the guiding light that directs the energy you raise and send out into the universe. If your intention was vague or ambiguous, the universe might also respond in a vague and ambiguous way.

For example, casting a spell to attract love into your life is a lovely intention, but what does love look like to you? Do you seek a romantic partner? Or do you wish to cultivate deeper friendships? Maybe you want to enhance self-love? When crafting your intention, be as specific and detailed as possible. Visualize exactly what you wish to manifest and infuse your spell with this vivid intention. If a spell didn't work, revisit your intention and see if it can be clarified or refined.

Furthermore, you might consider the timing of your spell. In Wicca, it's customary to align spells with lunar cycles, days of the week, or specific times of the day to maximize their effectiveness. Casting a spell for new beginnings during a waning moon, for instance, might not be as fruitful as casting it during a new moon. Also, remember that some spells might take time to manifest. The energies you've put out with your spell need time to work and align the right conditions for your intention to materialize.

You may also want to examine your emotional and mental state during the spellcasting. Were you feeling doubtful, distracted, or emotionally turbulent? Your mental and emotional energy can significantly impact the effectiveness of your spells. Spellcasting requires a calm mind, a focused intent, and an open heart. If you were feeling negative or chaotic emotions, these could have clouded your intention and scattered your energies.

Spellcasting is also about balance. When casting a spell, it's important to strike a balance between will and surrender. While it's crucial to have a strong will and desire for your intention to manifest, it's equally important to surrender the outcome to the divine powers that be. Clinging too tightly to a specific outcome or trying to control the how and when of its manifestation can restrict the flow of energy and potentially limit the ways your intention can materialize.

If your spell didn't work, it's also worth considering whether the spell was ethically sound. Remember the Wiccan Rede: "An it harm none, do what ye will." Spells that aim to manipulate others' free will, cause harm, or come from a place of greed or malice are unlikely to succeed and can even backfire. Make sure your spells always come from a place of love, respect, and for the good of all involved.

Lastly, know that sometimes, a spell may not work simply because it's not meant to be. This doesn't mean that you failed. Rather, it could be a sign that the intention of your spell is not in alignment with your highest good or the good of others. It's an invitation to revisit your intentions, reconsider your desires, and realign yourself with the universe's flow.

In the end, remember that spellcasting is a deeply personal and spiritual practice. It's a tool to connect with the divine energies of the universe, to manifest positive change, and to deepen your understanding of yourself and the world around you. Mistakes and challenges are part of the process, valuable opportunities to learn, grow, and refine your craft. Approach them with curiosity, patience, and an open heart. With time and practice, you'll become more attuned to the subtleties of energy work and more adept at casting effective, powerful spells.

An essential part of troubleshooting your spells involves paying close attention to your ritual environment. Were you able to maintain a sacred, undisturbed space during the spellcasting process? Distractions can interrupt the flow of energy and focus necessary for effective spellcasting. Perhaps you were disturbed by a phone call or a sudden noise. These distractions, while they might seem insignificant, can disrupt your concentration and the energy you've been building throughout the ritual. Ensuring you have a calm, quiet, and dedicated space for your spell work can significantly impact its success.

Moreover, take a moment to reflect on the tools and ingredients you used. Were they properly cleansed and consecrated? Each item used in a spell acts as a conduit for your intention and energy. If an item carries residual energy from past use or from others who have handled it, it can interfere with the purity of your intention. It is essential to cleanse all tools before using them in spellcasting. This can be done in various ways, including by smoke from sage or incense, by moonlight, or by burying them in the earth.

Your tools and ingredients also need to align with your intention. Each item in spellcasting, from herbs to crystals to candles, has unique symbolic properties. Using a rose quartz in a spell for financial prosperity might not be as effective as using a green aventurine, which is associated with wealth and abundance. Research and understand the symbolic meanings of your tools and ingredients to ensure they correspond with your intended outcome.

The words and actions you choose for your spell also matter. In spellcasting, words are not just mere utterances but powerful vibrational tools that can shape reality. If the words you chose didn't resonate with you or lacked conviction, they might not have carried the necessary power to project your intention into the universe. In future spell work, choose words that feel empowering and speak them with conviction and belief.

Likewise, every action in a spell is symbolic. The act of lighting a candle, for instance, can represent igniting your intention. If an action didn't resonate or feel meaningful, it might have weakened the spell. When creating a spell, every step should feel intuitively right and resonate with your personal belief system.

Understanding the flow of energy is fundamental to spellcasting. After casting the spell, did you ground your energy? Grounding is the process of releasing any surplus energy back into the earth, a step that signifies the completion of the spell. Failure to ground properly can result in feeling spacey or drained after a spell. Make sure to ground yourself after every spell by visualizing excess energy flowing down from your body and into the earth.

Another crucial element of effective spellcasting is patience. Change requires time. Once you have cast your spell and released your intention into the universe, have faith and be patient. Allow the universe the time to align circumstances in your favor. Constantly worrying about the results or becoming impatient can create energetic blocks that hinder the manifestation of your spell.

Lastly, keep a record of your spells in a Book of Shadows, or a magical diary. Note down the date, time, moon phase, your mood, the ingredients, and the exact words you used. If the spell did not work, you could refer to these notes and discern possible factors that could have affected its success.

In conclusion, remember that every spellcaster, even the most experienced, encounters spells that don't work as expected. It's a natural part of the learning process. Every failure is an opportunity to learn, to improve, and to deepen your understanding of your craft. With patience, practice, and the willingness to learn from your mistakes, you will find yourself growing not just as a spellcaster, but also as a Wiccan, continually evolving in your spiritual journey.

Creating Your Own Spells

As a practitioner of Wicca, you'll find that many of the spells you cast will be drawn from books, online resources, or passed down through traditions. However, as you grow more comfortable and knowledgeable in your practice, you may feel the call to create your own spells. The creation of your own spells allows for a deeper connection to the energies you work with and a personal touch to your magical workings. It may seem daunting at first, but this chapter aims to demystify the process and provide practical guidance on how to write your own spells.

When creating your own spells, the first step is always to clearly define your intention. What exactly is it that you hope to achieve? Whether it's love, protection, healing, prosperity, or something else entirely, having a clear and focused intention is vital. The more specific you can be, the better. Instead of aiming for something broad like "happiness," hone in on what that happiness would look like for you.

Is it a fulfilling relationship, a rewarding job, or a sense of inner peace and contentment?

However, it's essential to frame your intention positively and in the present tense, as if the desired outcome is already a reality. The universe responds to our thoughts and words as though they are occurring in the now, so instead of saying "I want to be free from anxiety," you might say, "I am filled with peace and calm." This is an important aspect to remember when formulating your intention.

Once you have your intention, the next step is to decide when to perform your spell. Timing can add a powerful boost to your spell-casting. You may choose to align your spell with the phases of the moon, the seasons, or a particular day of the week, each having different energies that can support your intention. For example, new moon energy is ideal for new beginnings and intentions, while the full moon is a time of power and fulfillment. A love spell might be best performed on a Friday, the day of Venus, the planet of love, while a spell for success could align with Sunday, the day of the Sun, representing power and success.

Your spell structure is the next aspect to consider. While spell structures can vary, they generally involve the following steps: cleansing and preparing your space, casting a circle, invoking deities or energies, stating your intention, raising energy, releasing your intention, and grounding. As you grow more experienced, you'll find a structure that suits you best. It's your spell, and it needs to resonate with you.

Now comes the fun part: choosing your tools and ingredients. These can include candles, herbs, crystals, symbols, oils, or anything else that feels right. The key is that each tool or ingredient should align with your intention and feel intuitively right to you. For example, you might choose a green candle for a prosperity spell or rose quartz for a love spell. This is where your research and learning come into play; every tool and ingredient has specific correspondences and energies.

The role of personal symbols and correspondences in spell creation cannot be overstated. These are potent tools that help your unconscious mind focus on the intention of your spell and tap into your inner power. Personal symbols can be anything that holds significant meaning for you, such as a specific animal, a shape, a number, a color, or even a piece of jewelry. When used in your spell, these symbols can serve as a powerful bridge between your conscious intention and your unconscious magical energy.

The process of creating your own spells is one of discovery, intuition, and deep personal connection to your magical practice. It involves connecting with the energies of the universe, harnessing them in harmony with your will, and directing them towards your goal. It's a deeply empowering and enriching process, and an integral part of your journey as a Wiccan.

Having discussed the basic structure and elements of a spell, we now delve further into how to imbue your spell with power and direction. Energy is at the heart of every spell, and understanding how to raise and direct it is crucial. While some people naturally have a stronger sense of their personal energy than others, everyone can develop and hone this skill with practice.

Just as intention is at the root of every spell, energy is the force that pushes the intention out into the universe. Think of it as the gasoline for your spell. Raising energy is often achieved through visualization. For instance, you might visualize a ball of light growing within you and with each breath, it gets brighter and more powerful. The color of this light might correspond to your intention—green for growth or prosperity, pink or red for love, blue for healing, and so forth.

There are also many other ways to raise energy. Chanting, drumming, dancing, or any repetitive physical action can help build up energy. The point is to reach a peak of energy that aligns with the peak of your emotional connection to your intention. Once you have raised this energy, you then visualize sending it out into the universe, or into the tool or ingredient you are working with, like a candle or a crystal.

The closing of your spell is just as important as the beginning. After releasing your energy and intention into the universe, it's crucial to ground yourself. This can be as simple as visualizing excess energy draining out of you and into the earth, eating a small snack, or taking a moment to sit quietly and breathe. Grounding brings you back to your normal state and seals your spell.

It's also customary to thank any deities or energies you have invoked and to close the circle you cast at the beginning of the spell. This is typically done by moving in the opposite direction to which it was cast, thanking the elements or deities for their presence and assistance, and visualizing the circle dissipating or being drawn back into your tool.

While the act of creating spells can be a highly personal and solitary practice, it's important to remember that you're not alone. The Wiccan community is a diverse and supportive one. It's perfectly normal and highly encouraged to seek advice, share experiences, and ask for guidance when you need it. The process of spell creation is a beautiful and complex dance between you, the energies you work with, and the universe.

When creating your own spells, don't be afraid to experiment. The effectiveness of a spell comes from your belief in it, your intention, and the energy you put into it, rather than the specific tools or words you use. Be open to trying new techniques, incorporating different tools, or using unconventional ingredients. Remember, what feels right for you and resonates with your intention is the most powerful component of your spell.

In the end, the creation of your own spells is a journey. There's no right or wrong way to do it, and it's not something that you'll perfect overnight. It's a continual process of learning, experimenting, and refining. The more you practice, the more intuitive and powerful your spell work will become.

The next part of this chapter will guide you further into this magical process, with more specific advice on how to bring your unique symbols and correspondences into your spell creation. Remember, this process should be enjoyable, empowering, and deeply personal. Let's continue our journey into the world of spell crafting.

Personal symbols and correspondences play a significant role in spell creation. As you've learned in the previous chapters, specific colors, herbs, crystals, and other tools have established correspondences within the Wiccan tradition. For instance, red is often associated with love and passion, lavender with peace and healing, and so forth. However, when it comes to creating your own spells, it's also crucial to consider your personal correspondences and symbols.

The power of a spell doesn't come from a candle, a crystal, or an incantation. It comes from you—the caster. Your energy, your intention, and your belief. Therefore, when you create your own spells, the materials and words you use should deeply resonate with you and your intentions.

If for you, the color blue has always symbolized love, then use a blue candle in your love spell. If a particular perfume or scent reminds you of abundance and prosperity, incorporate it into your prosperity spells. These personal symbols and correspondences, when aligned with your intention, can make your spells more potent because they have a personal significance to you and they can help to strengthen your focus and belief.

One way to uncover your personal correspondences is through meditation and introspection. Spend some time thinking about different symbols and what they mean to you. This doesn't have to be limited to physical objects or materials. Think about certain locations, animals, songs, or even memories that hold a significant meaning for you. All of these can be incorporated into your spells in one way or another.

Once you've determined your personal symbols and correspondences, it's time to bring them into your spell creation. This doesn't mean that you should disregard the traditional correspondences. In fact, using a blend of personal and traditional correspondences can often create a powerful and effective spell.

When incorporating your personal correspondences into a spell, ensure that they are integrated in a way that aligns with your intention. For example, if you're doing a spell to boost your self-confidence and you associate confidence with a particular song, you might play that song while preparing your spell or during the casting process.

In conclusion, crafting your own spells is a deeply personal and empowering process. It allows you to take control of your spiritual practice, to infuse your energy and intention into every aspect of your spell work, and to forge a deeper connection with the universe and the energies you're working with.

Remember, there's no 'right' or 'wrong' way to create a spell. What matters most is your intention, your belief, and your willingness to open yourself up to the magic of the universe. Whether you're drawing from time-honored traditions or blazing your own magical trail, the power is in your hands.

In the next chapter, we'll explore some advanced spellcasting techniques and delve into the world of magical timing, giving you more tools to enhance your spells and make your magical practice even more powerful. But for now, take some time to reflect on what you've learned in this chapter, and perhaps begin crafting a spell of your own. Remember, magic is a practice, and the more you engage with it, the more potent your spell work will become.

Conclusion

A s we come to the end of this enlightening journey, let's take a moment to look back and reflect on the rich tapestry of knowledge and wisdom that we've explored throughout this book. From understanding the fundamental principles and beliefs of Wicca, the reverence for nature, the worship of the deities, to the workings of the Wiccan Rede and Threefold Law, we've delved deeply into the spiritual core of this powerful religion. You've not only gained an appreciation for Wicca's harmony with nature and its ethical, empowering philosophies, but you've also begun to experience its magic firsthand through your spellwork.

In exploring the art of Wiccan spellcasting, we've gone beyond the mere mechanics of casting spells, recognizing that true magic comes from within – from our intention, focus, and belief. We've also looked at the tools of the trade, considering not just their physical properties, but their spiritual and symbolic significances as well. With each chapter, you've been given an array of spells to practice, experiment with, and incorporate into your daily life.

From enhancing your love life to improving your prosperity and well-being, you now have a spiritual toolkit that can help you navigate through life's challenges and celebrate its joys. Along the way, we've also examined important ethical considerations, reminding ourselves that the magic we wield should be done with respect for free will and an understanding of the responsibility it entails.

Importantly, we've debunked the myth that magic is an instant solution to life's problems. Rather, it's a path of personal empowerment, growth, and transformation. When a spell doesn't work as expected, it's not a failure, but an opportunity to learn, refine, and grow. And when you find yourself encountering challenges in your spellcasting journey, remember that this book has equipped you with the knowledge to troubleshoot and adjust your approach, to better align with your goals and the universe's energy.

We've also unlocked the magic of creating your own spells, giving you the freedom to personalize your craft and connect more deeply with your spells. Your understanding of personal and traditional symbols and correspondences will help you create spells that resonate strongly with your unique energy and intentions. As you continue your journey in Wicca, you will find that your spells will become increasingly powerful, and your relationship with the universe will grow ever more profound.

Wicca is not just a religion or a set of beliefs. It's a way of life, a path of spiritual growth, and a journey towards a deep connection with the divine energies that permeate our universe. And as with any journey, it's not about the destination, but the experiences, insights, and transformation we undergo along the way.

So, as we close this chapter, remember that the end of this book is not the end of your journey. It is, in fact, just the beginning.

As you proceed forward, let this knowledge guide you but not limit you. Wicca is a beautifully flexible faith, one that encourages individualism and personal connection with the divine. Remember, your journey is unique and the power of the universe is infinite, boundless. Embrace the magic within you and around you and allow it to shape your path.

Equally important is to bear in mind that every Wiccan's journey is personal and unique. Some may find a calling to solitary practice, while others may find fulfillment in the camaraderie of a coven. Be open to exploring different paths, and always follow your intuition. Magic is not a one-size-fits-all practice. It is deeply personal and unique to each practitioner.

Moreover, your path in Wicca does not end with mastery of spells or rituals. Indeed, the practice of magic is not the culmination but merely a facet of this spiritual journey. As you grow in your understanding and practice of Wicca, so will your capacity to connect with the universe and the divine energies within and around you.

Throughout this journey, I encourage you to maintain a sense of curiosity and an open mind. Continue exploring, learning, and experimenting. Keep refining your practices based on your experiences and the results of your spells. Reflect on your successes and challenges, learn from them, and use these insights to improve and strengthen your practice. Magic is a lifelong learning process, one that continually deepens and enriches your understanding of the universe and your place within it.

In the end, remember that Wicca and magic are not simply about manifesting our desires or wielding control over the world around us. They are about celebrating our connection with nature, tapping into the divine energies that flow through the universe, and harnessing these energies to create positive change in ourselves and the world around us.

The power to create change, to shape our reality, and to live in harmony with the natural world is not found in a spell, a ritual, or a tool. It is found within us. Wicca helps us uncover and tap into this innate power, guiding us towards a deeper, more profound understanding of our potential and our place in the universe.

As we wrap up this book, I hope that it has been enlightening and empowering. But more than that, I hope that it has ignited a flame within you – a flame of curiosity, of passion, and of reverence for the magical world of Wicca. Your journey has just begun, and the path ahead is filled with endless opportunities for growth, discovery, and transformation. Embrace it with open arms, an open heart, and an open mind. The magic awaits.

And so, with the closing of this book, we open the door to a new chapter of your life, one full of magic, mystery, and the beauty of Wicca. May your path be lit with the warm glow of enlightenment, your heart filled with love, and your soul with the comforting knowledge that you are a vital part of this beautiful, magical universe. Blessed Be.